Practice Tests Plus Volume 1 with key

B2 First

NEW EDITION

TEACHING
NOT JUST TESTING

T0345707

EXAM OVERVIEW

The **Cambridge English Qualification B2 First Exam,** also known as the **Cambridge First,** is made up of **four papers**, each testing different area of ability in English. The Reading and Use of English paper carries 40% of the marks, while Writing, Listening, and Speaking each carry 20% of the marks. There are five grades. A, B and C are pass grades; D and E are fail grades. Candidates also receive a numerical score on the Cambridge English scale for each skill.

Reading and Use of English	1 hour 15 minutes
Writing	1 hour 20 minutes
Listening	40 minutes (approximately)
Speaking	14 minutes (approximately) for each pair of students

All the examination questions are task-based. Rubrics (instructions) are important and should be read carefully. They set the context and give important information about the tasks. There is a separate answer sheet for recording answers for the Reading and Use of English and Listening papers.

Paper	Format	Task focus
Reading and Use of English 7 tasks 52 questions	**Part 1:** multiple-choice cloze. Choosing which word from a choice of four fits in each of eight gaps in the text.	Choice of vocabulary and relationships between words.
	Part 2: open cloze. Writing the missing word in each of eight gaps in the text.	Grammar, vocabulary and knowledge of expressions.
	Part 3: word formation. Choosing the form of the word given so that it fits into the gap in the text.	Grammatical accuracy and knowledge of vocabulary and expressions.
	Part 4: key-word transformations. Using the key word to complete a new sentence which means the same as the one given.	Grammatical accuracy and knowledge of vocabulary and sentence structure.
	Part 5: answering multiple-choice questions.	Reading for detailed understanding of text.
	Part 6: choosing which sentence fits into gaps in a text.	Reading to understand text structure.
	Part 7: deciding which of the short extracts or paragraphs contains given information or ideas.	Reading to locate specific information, detail, opinion and attitude.
Writing 2 tasks	**Part 1:** compulsory task, using given information to write an essay of 140-190 words.	Focus on writing for an English teacher in a formal style.
	Part 2: producing one piece of writing of 140-190 words, from one of the following: a letter, email, a report, a review or an article.	Focus on writing for a specific target reader, using appropriate layout and register.
Listening 4 tasks 30 questions	**Part 1:** eight short texts each with one multiple-choice question.	Understanding gist, detail, function, purpose, attitude, etc.
	Part 2: long text with ten sentence-completion questions.	Locating and recording specific information.
	Part 3: set of five short texts on a theme to match to one of eight prompts.	Understanding gist and main points.
	Part 4: long text with seven multiple-choice questions.	Understanding attitude, opinion, gist, main ideas and specific information.
Speaking 4 tasks	**Part 1:** examiner-led conversation.	Giving personal information.
	Part 2: individual long turn with visual and written prompts.	Organising discourse, describing, comparing, giving opinions.
	Part 3: two-way collaborative task with written prompts.	Sustaining interaction, expressing, justifying and eliciting ideas, agreeing and disagreeing.
	Part 4: three-way examiner-led discussion.	Expressing and justifying ideas, agreeing and disagreeing.

CONTENTS

Practice Test 1   **6**
Reading and Use of English   6
Writing   17
Listening   20
Speaking   25

Practice Test 2   **28**
Reading and Use of English   28
Writing   39
Listening   42
Speaking   47

Practice Test 3   **50**
Reading and Use of English   50
Writing   60
Listening   62
Speaking   66

Practice Test 4   **68**
Reading and Use of English   68
Writing   78
Listening   80
Speaking   84

Practice Test 5   **86**
Reading and Use of English   86
Writing   96
Listening   98
Speaking   102

Practice Test 6   **104**
Reading and Use of English   104
Writing   114
Listening   116
Speaking   120

Practice Test 7   **122**
Reading and Use of English   122
Writing   132
Listening   134
Speaking   138

Practice Test 8   **140**
Reading and Use of English   140
Writing   150
Listening   152
Speaking   156

Speaking and Writing bank   **158**
Speaking bank   158
Writing bank   162

Visuals for Speaking test   **169**
Test 1   169
Test 2   172
Test 3   175
Test 4   178
Test 5   181
Test 6   184
Test 7   187
Test 8   190

Answer key   **193**

GUIDANCE: READING AND USE OF ENGLISH

About the paper

The Reading and Use of English paper lasts for one-hour fifteen-minutes. There are seven parts and a total of fifty-two questions. You have to read texts of different lengths, for example extracts from newspapers, magazines, websites and novels, as well as other short texts. The paper tests your knowledge of vocabulary and grammar and your ability to read and understand different types of text.

Part 1

In Part 1, you read a short text and answer eight multiple-choice questions. There are eight gaps in the text and you have to choose a word or phrase from a choice of four. You choose the word or phrase which best fits each gap.

Part 2

In Part 2, you read a short text and answer eight open-cloze questions. There are eight gaps in the text. You have to fill each gap with the word that's missing.

Part 3

In Part 3, you read a short text and answer eight word-formation questions. There are eight gaps in the text and you're given the base form of each missing word. You have to change each word so that it makes sense in the gap.

Part 4

In Part 4, you read six pairs of sentences and answer key-word transformation questions. The pairs of sentences have the same meaning, but are expressed in different ways. There's a gap in the second sentence, which you have to fill with between two and five words. You're given one of these words.

How to do the paper

Part 1

- Read the text, ignoring the gaps, to get a general understanding.
- Only one of the options (A–D) fits the gap.
- Check the words before and after the gap, e.g. some words can only be followed by one preposition, or may be part of a common expression.
- In some questions, the answers are linking words and you need to understand the meaning of the whole text to know which answer is correct in the context.
- If you're not sure which answer to choose, decide which options are clearly wrong. Then look carefully at the ones that are left. If you're still not sure, you should guess. You don't lose marks for wrong answers, and your guess may be right.
- When you've finished, read the whole text again and check that it makes complete sense with your answers in the gaps.

Part 2

- Read the text, ignoring the gaps, to get a general understanding.
- Think about the missing words. You need to put one word in each gap and it's usually a grammatical word, e.g. pronoun, linker, preposition, etc.
- Before you fill each gap, read the sentence carefully and think about the type of word that's missing, e.g. it may be linking two ideas, or be part of a common expression.
- When you've finished, read the whole text again and check that it makes complete sense with your answers in the gaps.

Part 3

- Read the text, ignoring the gaps, to get a general understanding.
- Think about the missing words. You only need to put one word in each gap and the base form of that word is written in capital letters at the end of the line.
- Before you fill each gap, read the sentence carefully and think about the type of word that's missing, e.g. is it a noun, an adjective, an adverb, etc.?
- Change the word you've been given so that it fits the gap. You often need to add prefixes and suffixes.
- Check to see if nouns should be singular or plural.
- Check that you've spelled each new word correctly.
- When you've finished, read the whole text again and check that it makes complete sense with your answers in the gaps.

Part 4

- Read the first sentence carefully to make sure you understand exactly what it means.
- Look at the key word. What type of word is it? What usually follows it, e.g. an infinitive, a preposition, etc. Could it be part of a fixed expression or a phrasal verb?
- Remember you can't change the key word in any way.
- Now read the second sentence carefully. This sentence often has the same information as the first sentence, but expressed in a different order. Think about how the words need to change in the new order, e.g. an adjective may become a noun or vice versa.
- You can include words and phrases in your answer that aren't in the first sentence, but the meaning of the two sentences must be exactly the same.
- Check that your answer has between two and five words. Remember that contracted words count as two words, e.g. *won't* = *will not*.
- Check that the two sentences have exactly the same meaning as your answer in the gap.

About the paper

Part 5

In Part 5, you read one long text and answer six multiple-choice questions. There are four options in each question. The questions follow the order of information in the text.

Part 6

In Part 6, you read one long text from which six sentences have been removed. You can see these sentences, in jumbled order, below the text. There is also an extra sentence that doesn't fit into any of the gaps. You have to use your knowledge of grammar, vocabulary, referencing and text structure to decide which sentence fits in each gap.

Part 7

In Part 7, you read either one long text divided into sections, or a series of short texts on the same topic. There are ten questions, which report the information and ideas from the text(s). You have to match each question to the correct text or section of text.

How to do the paper

Part 5

- Read the text quickly to get a general understanding of what it's about and how it's organised.
- Read through the questions and underline key words.
- Find the section of text where the question is answered and read it carefully, underlining key words and phrases.
- Some questions test your knowledge of vocabulary or reference skills, and these tell you on which line the targeted word or phrase can be found. Read the sentences before and after the one including this word or phrase to find the answer.
- For all questions, read the four options (A–D) and choose the one that is closest to your own understanding of the text. Look for the same meaning expressed in different ways.
- Check that the other options are all clearly wrong. If you're still unsure, read the text again very carefully and look for reasons why some of the options are wrong.

Part 6

- Read the base text first, ignoring the gaps, to get a general understanding of what it's about and how it's organised.
- Then, read the text around each gap and think about what type of information might be missing.
- Read sentences A–G. Check for topic and language links with the base text. Highlight reference words and words that relate to people, places, events and any time references. This helps you to follow the development of the argument or narrative.
- Choose the best option to fit each gap. Make sure that all the pronouns and vocabulary references are clear.
- Once you've finished, re-read the whole text to be sure that it makes complete sense with your answers in the gaps.

Part 7

- In Part 7, you don't need to read the whole text first because you don't need to understand all the information in order to answer the questions.
- Read the questions (43–52) first, underlining key words and ideas.
- Read through the text(s) quickly and find information or ideas relevant to each question.
- For each question, read the relevant piece of text carefully to make sure it completely matches the meaning of the question.
- You'll probably find references to the ideas in the questions in more than one section of the text, but only one section matches the idea exactly. You need to read all these sections carefully to find the exact match.

Part 1

For questions **1 – 8**, read the text below and decide which answer (**A**, **B**, **C** or **D**) best fits each gap. There is an example at the beginning (**0**).

In the exam, you mark your answers **on a separate answer sheet**.

Example:

| 0 | **A** open | **B** free | **C** clear | **D** wide |

| 0 | A ▬ | B ▭ | C ▭ | D ▭ |

TIP STRIP

Question 3: This is a
fixed phrase. Which of
the options will make a
phrase that describes a
quantity?

Question 4: Which
of these words is
usually followed by the
preposition 'on'?

Question 6: Which
of these words usually
describes sunshine?

Question 8: Which
of these words can
be used instead of
'becoming'

Don't Forget your Hat

If you like spending time out in the (**0**) .... , it's important to remember that the human head doesn't work very well in hot, cold or wet conditions. That's why a hat is a good investment, and a single waterproof one with a brim will generally do the (**1**) .... adequately enough.

In cold climates, the head is (**2**) .... heat all the time. As (**3**) .... as sixty per cent of your body's heat is lost through the head and neck, (**4**) .... on which scientist you believe. Clearly this heat loss needs to be prevented, but it's important to remember that hats don't actually (**5**) .... you warm, they simply stop heat escaping.

Just as important is the need to protect the top of your head and your neck from the effects of (**6**) .... sunlight, and the brim of your hat will do this. If you prefer a baseball cap, (**7**) .... buying one that has a drop down 'tail' at the back to stop your neck (**8**) .... sunburnt.

1	**A** job	**B** task	**C** role	**D** duty
2	**A** giving away	**B** sending out	**C** dropping off	**D** running down
3	**A** soon	**B** long	**C** well	**D** much
4	**A** according	**B** regarding	**C** depending	**D** relating
5	**A** maintain	**B** stay	**C** hold	**D** keep
6	**A** sharp	**B** keen	**C** bright	**D** deep
7	**A** consider	**B** recommend	**C** advise	**D** suggest
8	**A** suffering	**B** going	**C** having	**D** getting

For questions **9 – 16**, read the text below and think of the word which best fits each gap. Use only **one** word in each gap. There is an example at the beginning (**0**).

In the exam, you write your answers **IN CAPITAL LETTERS on a separate answer sheet**.

Example: | 0 | W | H | E | N | | | | | | | | | | | | | | |

Penguins on the move

For years, the penguins at San Francisco zoo led a relatively quiet life. They'd only get excited and swim around at mealtimes, **(0)** .... fish was always provided for them.

Then one day, six new penguins, **(9)** .... had been entertaining visitors to a theme park, arrived to share their pool. These new arrivals immediately dived in to show **(10)** .... their swimming skills. Ever **(11)** .... that moment, the pool has been alive with fifty-two birds swimming around non-stop, **(12)** .... if they were setting off on a long journey.

At first, this behaviour puzzled the zookeepers. Scientists, **(13)** .... , have the answer. Penguins are very social and inquisitive birds, and the arrival of new individuals in a group always creates a lot of interest. In the wild, penguins of this type typically swim thousands of miles each year **(14)** .... search of food, and it **(15)** .... thought that the newcomers may **(16)** .... reawakened the migratory instinct in the San Francisco birds.

TIP STRIP

Question 9: Which relative pronoun is needed here?

Question 13: Which linking word is needed here?

Question 14: Which is the correct preposition to complete the expression?

Question 15: A verb form is needed to complete the passive form. Which tense will it be in?

Part 3

For questions **17 – 24**, read the text below. Use the word given in capitals at the end of some of the lines to form a word that fits in the gap **in the same line**. There is an example at the beginning (**0**).

In the exam, you write your answers **IN CAPITAL LETTERS on a separate answer sheet**.

Example:

| 0 | F | A | S | C | I | N | A | T | I | O | N | | | | | | | |

TIP STRIP

Question 17: Is a noun or an adjective needed here?

Question 21: What is the noun made from this adjective? Be careful of your spelling.

Question 22: This word needs a prefix. Both negative and positive prefixes exist, which do you need here?

Question 23: Will this word be positive or negative? How do you know?

The sky at night

For anyone with a **(0)** .... for the study of the night sky, Hawaii is one of the best places to get a clear view of the stars and planets. Because it is a **(17)** .... area, situated in the middle of a large expanse of ocean, Hawaii is much less affected by light **(18)** .... than most other parts of the world. If you are **(19)** .... enough to go to the top of the dormant volcano known as Mauna Kea, the view is even more **(20)** .... The volcano, which rises to a **(21)** .... of 4205 metres is one of the best places in the world to get **(22)** .... views of the night sky and therefore is the location for more than a dozen of the world's finest telescopes.

Of special significance is the WM Keck Observatory which has a pair of extremely large and **(23)** .... telescopes. In recent years these telescopes have been responsible for the **(24)** .... of many new planets beyond our solar system.

FASCINATE

MOUNTAIN

POLLUTE

FORTUNE

IMPRESS

HIGH

INTERRUPTED

POWER

DISCOVER

Part 4

For questions **25 – 30**, complete the second sentence so that it has a similar meaning to the first sentence, using the word given. **Do not change the word given**. You must use between **two** and **five** words, including the word given. Here is an example (**0**).

Example:

0   What type of music do you like best?

FAVOURITE

What .... type of music?

The gap can be filled with the words 'is your favourite', so you write:

Example: | **0** | *IS YOUR FAVOURITE*

In the exam, you write **only** the missing words **IN CAPITAL LETTERS on a separate answer sheet.**

TIP STRIP

Question 25: A passive verb form is needed. Remember to keep the tense the same.

Question 26: Which common expression about the future uses the word 'forward'?

Question 27: A noun is needed after 'my'.

Question 28: You need to make the key word negative in your answer.

Question 30: Is the key word followed by a gerund or an infinitive?

25   They are opening a new branch of that bookshop in our town

BEING

A new branch of that bookshop .... in our town.

26   Patrick can't wait to see the team's next home game.

FORWARD

Patrick is really .... the team's next home game.

27   Denise said that she'd always intended to invite Phil to the party.

MY

'It had always .... invite Phil to the party,' said Denise.

28   Paolo damaged his brother's digital camera by accident.

MEAN

Paolo .... his brother's digital camera.

29   Suzy says she will only play tennis if Fiona plays with her.

UNLESS

Suzy has refused .... plays with her.

30   People think that the famous actress will arrive in the city this morning.

EXPECTED

The famous actress .... in the city this morning.

You are going to read an extract from an article about a car rally in the desert. For questions **31 – 36**, choose the answer (**A**, **B**, **C** or **D**) which you think fits best according to the text.

In the exam, you mark your answers **on a separate answer sheet**.

Driving in the Desert

My family are farmers in France. By the age of ten, I could manoeuvre a tractor into a field to pick up straw bales. For my driving test, I learned how to reverse into a parking space by practising between two tractors. I've always needed to prove that I can adapt to new situations. I'd never left France until I did a gap year in Australia, the most distant country possible. I worked on a sheep farm there, driving a 4WD vehicle all the time, and spent four months driving around the country on my own. That was when I first came into contact with the desert, and I wanted to return to it.

But it was my competitive spirit that drew me to the all-female Gazelles Rally. I did it to see if I could survive in desert conditions and not be afraid. Taking part in the rally involves spending eight days in the desert, including two sets of two-day marathons when you're on your own overnight with your team-mate. The rally pushes you to the limits of your physical and mental capacity, so it's very important to choose the right team-mate, to make sure you have the same goal and the same way of working. But the key thing is for you both to keep your courage and remain confident.

Participants – known as the *gazelles* – drive 4WDs, quad bikes, motorbikes or trucks, and use a compass and a map to navigate their way to marker flags that have been planted in the desert – always in places that are really difficult to get at. You have to drive up and down huge sand dunes, the highest of which are about twenty metres. Every morning at base camp you have to prepare your maps, by marking the position of the day's flags. Then you have to plan the best route to them. It takes time to learn how to do this, how to understand the landscape, because you're all alone in the emptiness

– there are no landmarks, it's all just flat. On our first day, my team-mate and I felt quite frightened by it – we thought we'd get lost. So we decided to drive in a straight line for half an hour in search of geographical features. Then we found some mountains.

It rained a lot during the rally, and the thing that scared us most was the thought of being unable to get out of the mud. Some women were stuck for about twelve hours overnight before the mud dried. We managed to get through, though, because we set off first, when the ground was less damaged. Each vehicle carries a satellite tracking system with it, and every half-hour the rally organisers use this to check on you: if a car isn't moving, they go to the rescue. Once we were all alone in our tent in a storm, and feeling a bit scared. An official rally vehicle came and reassured us that we wouldn't be washed away.

I had great difficulty finding a sponsor – it costs a lot to hire a vehicle and enter the rally, plus you have to hire safety equipment. It's always the people you least expect who help you most. The big dealers for four-wheel-drive vehicles refused to finance what they called 'a girls' jaunt in the desert'. It was a small, independent garage that provided us with an 11-year-old 4WD for nothing – and we didn't have a single breakdown.

Speed isn't a factor in this competition. Men have a tendency to drive a bit faster than women. They're so sure they've chosen the right route that they're less good at anticipating problems. A man who was doing a television programme on the rally refused to believe that it was difficult or that women could sometimes do it better. I want to do the rally again next year – it puts life's everyday problems into perspective.

31 Why did the writer go to Australia?

A to further develop her driving skills

B to get practice in driving in desert conditions

C to visit members of her family who farmed there

D to experience living in an unfamiliar environment

32 In the writer's opinion, the ideal rallying team-mate is someone who

A keeps you from feeling afraid at night.

B shares your general aims and attitudes.

C doesn't take the competition too seriously.

D can make up for any weaknesses you have.

33 What does the word 'this' in line **34** refer to?

A drawing flags on a map

B driving in difficult places

C finding important landmarks

D deciding which route to take

34 The writer's greatest fear in the desert was that she might

A lose her way in bad weather.

B become stuck in wet ground.

C damage her vehicle in the mud.

D have to be rescued by other competitors.

35 What does the writer say about the cost of the rally?

A Hiring a vehicle was her biggest expense.

B Safety equipment was provided by the organisers.

C She was surprised that a small garage sponsored her.

D A new vehicle would have reduced her maintenance bill.

36 According to the writer, men rally drivers

A fail to realise when something is about to go wrong.

B tend to feel overconfident when driving at speed.

C seem to have fewer problems with navigation.

D refuse to accept the advice of women.

TIP STRIP

Question 31: Read the text carefully. What did she know before she went and what did she discover when she got there?

Question 33: Look before the pronoun to find out what it took time to learn.

Question 34: Find another way of saying 'greatest fear' in the text.

You are going to read an article about exercising to music. Six sentences have been removed from the article. Choose from the sentences **A – G** the one which fits each gap (**37 – 42**). There is one extra sentence you do not need to use.

In the exam, you mark your answers **on a separate answer sheet**.

Music to get fit by

A fitness trainer argues that music can increase our workout productivity

I used to go to the gym regularly, but I never liked the music they played there. I always associate physical activity with music belting out at 140 beats per minute, and I trained as an instructor largely so that I'd have control of the audio. This isn't as crazy as it sounds. Music and exercise have long been known to be close companions. Dr Costas Karageorghis, a sports and exercise psychologist who's also a musician, has been studying the link between athletic activity and music.

Karageorghis says we have an underlying predisposition to react to musical stimuli. 'Music is beneficial,' he explains, 'because of the similarities between rhythm and human movement. The synchronisation of music with exercise consistently demonstrates increased levels of work output among exercise participants.' **37**

For one Olympic rower, the ideal music was a Red Hot Chili Peppers' album, which he says played an integral part in his preparation for the games. **38** If you aren't familiar with this word, it means that during repetitive exercise, music essentially diverts attention away from the sensation of fatigue. The right music can almost persuade your body that you are in fact having a nice sit down and a coffee.

Not everyone, however, shares the same taste in tunes. 'Can you turn that racket down?' said a participant in one of my classes before storming out. Reaching a consensus on music is notoriously tricky – which makes communal exercise classes problematic. There are, however, some rules that professional fitness instructors follow. **39**

Most importantly, however, the music should mirror your heartbeat. The instructor should choose the music to go with the different phases of a class, from the warm up, to high intensity, to the final relaxing phase. It's advisable to follow this sequence when you're working out alone, too, and not make the mistake a good friend of mine made. **40**

Instructors and gyms often buy ready-mixed compilations that come with a music licence, without which they can be fined heavily. A frequent complaint by those who go to classes is that they hear the same old songs over and over again. **41** It's also true, sadly, that most people respond best in motivational terms to quite awful songs – music they wouldn't necessarily be proud to have on their playlist.

42 In order to prepare mentally, for example, golfers can get hold of a special range of music just for them. Whatever your sport, I'd like to give you some final words of advice. As Karageorghis suggests, enjoy the beat and let the music motivate you, but never forget your main objective is to exercise and music is only there to help you do that.

A But perhaps the most useful thing about music is that it allows even the humble gym-goer or runner to practise a technique used by elite athletes, known as 'disassociation'.

B These days you can find music tailored to suit an incredibly diverse range of sports and exercise needs.

C One of them is that the music must be appropriate to the type of class and not just the instructor's personal enthusiasm for a particular genre or artist.

D This is mostly because only a limited number of them are released for public performance each year, and partly because teachers universally favour the most popular tracks.

E The most convenient is the gym called Third Space in London's Soho, which does several sessions a week to live DJ accompaniment.

F He was cooling down to techno music, which left him feeling nervous and twitchy all day.

G Choose the right music and, according to Karageorghis, you can up your workout productivity by as much as twenty per cent.

TIP STRIP

Question 38: The gap is followed by 'familiar with this word'. Can you find a word that needs explaining in the sentences?

Question 39: The sentence before the gap mentions 'some rules'. Can you find a sentence that gives an example of a rule?

Question 40: You need to find a sentence that describes the mistake that was made.

Part 7

You are going to read an article about four people who write blogs. For questions **43 – 52**, choose from the bloggers (**A – D**). The bloggers may be chosen more than once.

In the exam, you mark your answers **on a separate answer sheet**.

Which blogger . . .

started writing the blog as a way of improving career prospects?	**43**

mentions using a personal blog in professional activities?	**44**

warns prospective bloggers about a loss of privacy?	**45**

made a decision to improve the quality of the blog?	**46**

is unconcerned about making mistakes in the blog?	**47**

felt no need to learn anything new before starting to write blogs?	**48**

initially doubted that readers would be attracted to the blog?	**49**

compares the ease of writing blogs to other types of writing?	**50**

values the fact that the blog provides a break from work?	**51**

remembers other people being less open about what they had written?	**52**

TIP STRIP

Question 43: Bloggers A, C and D all tell us about their jobs – but which one says blogging could help in that career?

Question 45: Look for a word that means 'nobody knows who you are'

Question 50: Bloggers A and D both mention blogging and other types of writing, but which one makes a comparison that focuses on how easy it is to do.

Why do people start writing blogs?

Read the personal stories of four bloggers.

A Ann Handley

Like many of my school friends, I used to spend hours every day writing a diary in a little book. But while they kept theirs hidden under their beds, I needed an audience, interaction and feedback. One day, my teacher encouraged me to join a pen-friend organisation and I used to write pages of fascinating detail about my teacher, my friends, my dog … I even invented a few personalities, the details of which were far more interesting than my own life. So when one of my colleagues explained to me what blogging was all about – the frequent postings, the feedback, the trackbacks, I felt confident that I already knew all about it. I'm now a marketing specialist and my blog is a business tool. But at the same time I'm reliving the joy of communicating and the thrill of the conversation.

B Dave Armano

A year ago I was a professional minding my own business. When I started reading blogs, I would say to myself: 'There's so much information out there – so many smart people.' I decided to start my own blog, but I had no idea what I was doing. I was basically a nobody and I was trying to get people to listen to me. What was I thinking? But then I created a visual for my blog and before I knew it, I had all these other blogs linking to me – doing weird stuff like trackbacks. I had no idea what a trackback was, but I went from forty hits a day to close to a hundred overnight. It was amazing! That's when I stopped to think: if I wanted traffic, I needed to get some good content there, and that's what really worked for me.

C Carol Krishner

It's great to have my personal blog because I feel free and if I make mistakes I learn from the experience. I'm a lecturer, and it's refreshing to be able to step outside my academic interests and into a different world. But it's interesting that when you choose topics to write about you give others hints about yourself, and people do get to know you. So it's not the thing to do if you want to remain anonymous. One of the first lessons I learned is that the blogosphere is a genuine community. After asking a question in a blog comment about what qualities are needed in a good blog, I soon got spot-on advice from a blogger I didn't even know. Then I had an invitation to a local face-to-face blogger meet-up, which was an amazing experience.

D Debbie Weil

I started my first blog exactly three years ago for a very practical reason. It was clear to me that blogs were going to become a useful tool in my future job as a journalist. I needed to know how to use this new tool, and I figured blogging myself was the quickest way to get up to speed. I learnt quickly and since then I've helped others launch their own personal blogs. The simplicity of blogging software enables me to write short entries without any problems or delays. Writing a 750-word article is a daunting task, but a quick blog entry takes less than a minute. And yet the effect is so significant – I get calls from companies saying they've read my blog and would I be available to give a presentation, for a large fee.

GUIDANCE: WRITING

About the paper

The paper lasts for 1 hour and 20 minutes. There are two parts to the paper and in each part you have to complete one task.

Part 1

Part 1 is compulsory. You have to write an essay in a formal style, giving your opinion on the essay title, using the ideas given and providing an idea of your own. You should write between 140 and 190 words.

Part 2

In Part 2, you must choose one question from a choice of three. Tasks may include some of the following: an article, an email, a letter, a report or a review. You should write between 140 and 190 words.

Task types
- Letter or email
- Article
- Report
- Review

For more information about the writing paper task types, refer to the Writing Bank on pages 162–168

How to do the paper

Part 1

- Don't be in a hurry to start writing. It pays to spend a few minutes planning! Read the instructions carefully to understand:
- – the topic you had discussed in class and the title of the essay you have to write
  – what information you have to include in your answer: this will ensure that you include the two notes provided.
- Think of a third point of your own, something which is not mentioned in the first two points given.
- Look again at the three written notes and expand them by noting down a couple of ideas for each.
- Decide how many paragraphs you will need and which ideas you want to group together in each paragraph.
- When you finish, do a final check. Is the style formal or semi-formal? Have you included all the notes? Are there any basic mistakes that you can correct?

Part 2

- Remember that whereas in Part 1 you always have to write an essay in a formal style, in Part 2 you need to choose from task types that may require a semi-formal or informal style, and a variety of formats.
- Don't be in hurry to start writing. Look carefully at each task (e.g. the report) and topic (e.g. a sports centre) and:
  – Think of report writing. Are you confident you know how to write the task type?
  – Think of a sports centre as a topic. Do you have some interesting language you can use?
- Choose a topic where your answers to both these questions is 'yes'. For example, choose the report only if you know how to present and organise the information, and you also like the topic and have some interesting language you can use.
- Read the task you have chosen and be sure you understand the following:
  – What is the situation?
  – Who will read your piece of writing?
  – What is your purpose in writing this piece?
- Jot down the ideas that come into your head, in any order. Then choose your best ideas and decide how you will organise them into paragraphs.
- When you finish, revise your writing. Have you used varied language? Are your points clearly expressed?

You **must** answer this question. Write your answer in **140 – 190** words in an appropriate style.

1   In your English class you have been discussing the use of communication technology such as phones and tablets in our everyday lives. Now your English teacher has asked you to write an essay.

Write an essay using **all** the notes and giving reasons for your point of view.

Can we live happily without using communication technology all the time?

Notes

Write about:

1. phones or other devices we can't live without

2. to use or not to use phones in certain social situations

3. .... (your own idea)

TIP STRIP

*   Begin by underlining the key words in the instructions, e.g. 'phones and tablets in our everyday life', 'using all the notes'.
*   Read the essay question and the two written prompts. Note down a couple of ideas to include for each prompt, and also some interesting vocabulary you can use. For example, for the second prompt, you could jot down 'turn off your phone', 'avoid checking messages'. Think of a third idea of your own and make some notes on that too.
*   Plan your answer. Decide which ideas to include in each paragraph. Remember that writing an essay is much easier when you have a plan!
*   Introduce the topic in the first paragraph. You can do this by rephrasing the essay question, for example: 'Some people would say they can't be happy unless they use their phones all the time.'
*   Try to use a variety of tenses and grammatical structures. Don't forget to summarise your opinions briefly in the last paragraph.
*   When you've finished, check that you've dealt with the two notes provided and added a point of your own. Check that you've written between 140 and 190 words, but don't waste time counting every word.
*   Finally, check your grammar and spelling.

Part 2

Write an answer to one of the questions **2 – 4** in this part. Write your answer in **140 – 190** words in an appropriate style.

2   You have seen an announcement in an international magazine.

> # MY CHILDHOOD FRIEND
> Tell us about your best friend when you were a child and say why you got on well together.
> **The best article will win a book.**

Write your **article**.

3   You have seen this advertisement for a part-time job and you want to apply.

> # World Tours Agency
> We need a young person to show a group of English-speaking teenagers round this area.
>
> Are you the energetic and sociable person we're looking for?
> Are you available in August?   Are you fluent in English?   Do you get on well with teenagers?
> *Write to* **Sam Bastion**, **the manager**.

Write your **letter**.

4   A new sports centre opened recently in your area and a community website has asked you to write a report, giving your opinions about the following:
   • how good the facilities for the more popular sports are.
   • how welcoming the reception staff and sports trainers are.
   • what the prices for students and other people are like.

Write your **report**.

TIP STRIP

• Choose a question you have the ideas and vocabulary for.
• Underline key points in the question and use them in your answer.
• Before you start writing, think about what type of task it is. Note down the main point to include in each paragraph.
• Think about how you can organise your ideas.
• Remember to check your spelling and grammar.
Question 2:
• Introduce your topic in the first paragraph and summarise what you've said in the last paragraph.
• Describe your friend and say why you got on well.
• Try to use varied language and avoid repeating adjectives.
Question 3:
• Will your style be formal or informal? You could write 3 paragraphs, covering the points you've been given.
Question 4:
• You could use a heading for each part.
• Jot down some vocabulary, before writing.

GUIDANCE: LISTENING

About the paper

The Listening Paper lasts about 40 minutes and has four parts, with a total of thirty questions. You listen to texts of different types and different lengths, e.g. extracts from presentations, media broadcasts and announcements, as well as everyday conversations. You hear each recording twice, and you have time to read the questions before you listen.

Part 1

In Part 1, you listen to eight unrelated extracts of around half a minute each. The extracts may be monologues or dialogues and include a range of speakers and contexts. You have to answer one three-option multiple-choice question on each extract. Each question tests a slightly different listening skill, for example you may be asked to identify a speaker's main point, opinion, feeling or attitude, or whether two speakers agree with each other.

Part 2

In Part 2, you listen to one long monologue of around 3 minutes. The speaker is usually giving a presentation on a specific topic. A set of ten sentences reports the speaker's main points. A word or short phrase has been removed from each sentence. You have to listen and complete the gaps. This task tests your ability to find and record specific information in the listening text.

Part 3

In Part 3, you hear a series of five short monologues of around 30 seconds each. Each of the five speakers is talking about the same topic. As you listen, you look at a list of eight options and decide which one matches what you hear. There are three options you do not need to use. This task tests your ability to understand the gist of what people are saying.

Part 4

In Part 4, there is one long text of around 3 minutes. This is generally an interview or a discussion between two people. You have to listen and answer seven three-option multiple-choice questions. This task tests your detailed understanding of the interview, including the main speaker's attitudes, feelings and opinions.

How to do the paper

Part 1

- The eight extracts are not linked in any way. There's a variety of situations and speakers, e.g. announcements, informal conversations, etc.
- Before you listen to each extract, look at the context sentence. Think about who the speaker is, the topic and the context, e.g. is it part of a radio programme, an informal chat, etc.?
- Some questions ask you to identify the speakers' opinions. Before you listen, think about which of the speakers you're listening for in each question and underline key words in the question stem. Some questions focus on both speakers and whether they agree or not.
- Some questions ask you to identify a speaker's feeling or attitude, or that person's purpose in talking, e.g. to explain, to apologise, etc.
- Some questions test your understanding of a speaker's main idea, or a detailed piece of information that they give.
- The first time you listen, find the correct answer to the question posed in the stem.
- Then listen again to match that answer to the correct option (A–C).
- The words in the questions and options don't use the same vocabulary and expressions as the speakers on the recordings. You need to match the meaning of ideas expressed in the recording to the wording of the questions.

Part 2

- Before you listen, read the context sentence. Think about the person who's speaking and the topic you're going to hear about.
- You have 1 minute to read through the sentences before you listen. Think about the type of information that is missing in each sentence.
- Most answers are concrete pieces of information, e.g. proper nouns.
- The sentences that you read are in the same order as the information you hear. Use the sentences to help you keep your place as you listen.
- You hear the words you need to write on the recording. There's no need to change the form of the words or to find a paraphrase.
- You won't hear the exact sentences that you read, but you will hear the same ideas and some of the same vocabulary. Listen for the key words and ideas in the sentence.

- Write no more than three words in each gap. Most answers are single words or compound nouns.
- Check that your answer fits grammatically, e.g. singular and plural, tense, etc. and that it makes sense in the complete sentence.

Part 3

- Before you listen, you hear the context sentence. Think about the topic and what you have to listen for.
- There are five different speakers all talking about the same topic. You hear all five of them once and then the whole set is repeated.
- You have time to read the questions before you listen. Read the options (A–H) so that you're ready to choose one as you listen to each speaker.
- The first time you listen, pay attention to the speaker's main idea. Mark the option closest to this idea. Remember that the five speakers are all talking about the same topic, so you'll hear the same vocabulary and similar information from each speaker.
- The second time you listen, check your answers. You may need to change some of them. Remember that there are three options that you don't need to use.
- Don't worry if you don't understand every word. If you're not sure of an answer, then guess. You've probably understood more than you think.

Part 4

- Before you listen, read the context sentence. Think about the people who are speaking and the topic you're going to hear about.
- You have 1 minute to read through the questions before you listen.
- Underline the key words in each question stem and options.
- The questions follow the order of information you hear when you listen. Listen out for key vocabulary and ideas that introduce the topic of each question. These are often in the interviewer's question.
- The first time you listen, find the correct answer to the question.
- Then listen again to match that answer to the correct option (A–C).
- The words in the questions and options don't use the same vocabulary and expressions as the speakers on the recording. You need to match the meaning of ideas expressed in the recording to the wording of the questions.

You will hear people talking in eight different situations. For questions **1 – 8**, choose the best answer (**A**, **B** or **C**).

1   You hear a woman recommending a campsite.
Why does she recommend it?
A   It's close to tourist attractions.
B   It's in an area of natural beauty.
C   It has a wide range of facilities.

2   You hear two friends talking about global warming.
How does the woman feel about it?
A   pessimistic about the future
B   surprised at the effects it's having
C   unconvinced that there's a problem

3   You hear a young couple talking about moving to the country.
The man objects to the idea because
A   he wouldn't be able to work there.
B   he'd miss the facilities of the city.
C   he wouldn't be near to his friends.

4   You hear a part of a radio programme about food.
Why should listeners call the programme?
A   to take part in a recipe competition
B   to find out about a cookery course
C   to ask questions about cooking

5   You hear the beginning of a programme about college canteens.
What point is being made about them?
A   The choice of food has improved.
B   Students like the food on offer there.
C   Teachers complain about the quality of the food.

6   You hear a young woman talking about her career.
She accepted a job in a bookshop because
A   she needed a steady income.
B   she thought it would be enjoyable.
C   she hoped to improve certain skills.

7   You hear part of a programme about a clothes designer.
What does the woman like about the clothes he designs?
A   They are practical.
B   They are colourful.
C   They are original.

8   You hear a discussion about the sport of snow-kiting.
What does the man say about it?
A   It's easier to learn than other winter sports.
B   It's more dangerous than other winter sports.
C   It requires less equipment than other winter sports.

TIP STRIP

Question 1: She mentions a tourist attraction (castle) and facilities (showers), but these aren't why she recommends the campsite.

Question 2: You're listening for the woman's opinion, but the man's response to what she says will also help you to get the answer.

Question 4: Think about the question. What are you listening for? The word 'call' comes at the end of the recording, but you need to understand what comes before it to answer the question.

Question 6: Be careful. The last thing she talks about is money (income), but is this the answer to the question?

You will hear a programme about a boy called Michael who crossed the Atlantic in a sailing boat. For questions **9 – 18**, complete the sentences with a word or short phrase.

Sailing solo across the Atlantic

To achieve his record, Michael had to sail a total of

(9) .... kilometres without any help.

Michael helped to design his boat which was called

(10) ....

Michael and his father were concerned in case any

(11) .... came too close to them.

All the food that Michael took on his voyage

was in (12) .... bought at the supermarket.

The type of food which Michael missed most on the trip was

(13) ....

Michael enjoyed using his (14) ....

to keep track of what his father was doing.

Michael's favourite pastimes on the boat were using his sister's

(15) .... and reading.

Michael got a fright when a (16) .... landed on him.

The name of the charity that Michael is raising funds for is

(17) ....

When Michael sails round the world, he plans to take

(18) .... with him in case he feels homesick.

TIP STRIP

Question 9: What type of information are you listening for? A word, a number or the name of something?

Question 11: Think about the type of things that might come close to the boat, then listen to hear if any of these is the answer.

Question 13: Listen carefully, more than one type of food is mentioned, but which did Michael miss most?

Question 17: Make sure you write down the full name of the charity.

Question 18: What would you take on this type of trip? Listen to see if Michael has the same idea.

Part 3

You will hear five short extracts in which people are talking about cookery courses. For questions **19 – 23**, choose from the list (**A – H**) what each speaker says about the course they took. There are three extra letters which you do not need to use.

A   It helped me to renew my enthusiasm for cooking.

B   It gave me ideas for improving my own recipes.

Speaker 1 | 19 |

C   It took into account the fact that I wasn't a beginner.

Speaker 2 | 20 |

D   It required me to do things rather than just watch.

Speaker 3 | 21 |

E   It gave me skills I wish I'd acquired earlier in life.

Speaker 4 | 22 |

F   It included an unexpected search for ingredients.

Speaker 5 | 23 |

G   It focused too much on one particular type of food.

H   It taught me how to use the latest kitchen equipment.

TIP STRIP

Sometimes you hear the words in the options in the recordings, but this may not be the answer, for example:

A: Speakers 2 and 4 both talk about enthusiasm but neither of them talks about 'renewing' it.

B: Speaker 4 mentions 'equipment', but doesn't say it's the latest.

E: Speakers 1–5 all talk about learning new skills, but which speaker is unhappy about not learning these earlier in life?

F: The word 'ingredients' is mentioned by Speakers 1 and 5, but neither of them mentions searching for ingredients.

You will hear an interview with a fashion designer called Pamela Green. For questions **24 – 30**, choose the best answer (**A**, **B** or **C**).

24   What helped Pamela to decide to become a fashion designer?

  A   working as an assistant in a fashion shop
  B   doing research into the fashion industry
  C   attending a course on fashion design

25   What does Pamela say about having a degree in fashion?

  A   It's essential for promotion.
  B   It's evidence of your ability.
  C   It guarantees you a better income.

26   Pamela says that when starting your own fashion label, it's most important to

  A   enjoy the creative process.
  B   contact shops that might sell it.
  C   have a business plan.

27   Where does Pamela usually find inspiration for her fashion designs?

  A   in the work of other designers
  B   in the styles of other countries
  C   in the clothes her friends wear

28   What aspect of her work does Pamela find most difficult to deal with?

  A   the pressure to meet deadlines
  B   the failure of some of her designs
  C   the need to attend fashion shows

29   According to Pamela, successful designers need to be able to

  A   predict future fashions.
  B   recognise all past styles.
  C   get their designs published.

30   What advice does Pamela have for people who want a career in fashion?

  A   be aware of the options available
  B   don't be afraid of sudden fame
  C   learn from your own errors

TIP STRIP

Question 24: Listen for another way of saying 'decided', the answer comes soon after this.

Question 26: Read the question. Remember you're listening for what Pamela thinks is 'most important'.

Question 27: The interviewer uses the word 'inspiration'. Listen to what Pamela says in answer to his question to find the answer.

Question 29: 'According to Pamela' means 'in Pamela's opinion' – listen for what she thinks makes a designer successful.

Question 30: Listen to the whole of Pamela's last turn. What is her main message?

GUIDANCE: SPEAKING

About the paper

The Speaking Test contains four parts and lasts 14 minutes. There are two candidates and two examiners. One examiner acts as interlocutor and interacts with the candidates and the other examiner acts as assessor and does not join the conversation. The candidates are assessed on their performance over the whole test.

Part 1 (2 minutes)

The examiner asks candidates questions about their own lives, focusing on areas such as their daily life, leisure, work, future plans, holidays, likes and dislikes. The examiner addresses each candidate in turn and does not invite them to talk to each other, though the candidates may do so if they wish. This is a natural way to begin the test and it allows candidates to settle and feel comfortable.

Part 2 (4 minutes)

Each candidate is given the opportunity to speak for 1 minute without interruption. The interlocutor gives each candidate two pictures and reads out a task. One part of this task is to compare them, but there is also an extra task which is written above the pictures. At the end of each long turn, the examiner asks the other candidate a question which only requires a brief answer.

Part 3 (4 minutes)

Both candidates are given oral instructions and a diagram with one question and five written prompts, which is the basis for the task that they have to carry out together. The instructions are in two parts. First the examiner will ask the candidates to talk to each other about the question and the different written prompts. The written question helps candidates focus on the task. The candidates will be given 15 seconds to look at the task before starting the discussion. Then, after two minutes, the examiner will give the candidates 1 minute to decide on something. When making their decision, candidates will be expected to give reasons for their choices.

Part 4 (4 minutes)

The examiner asks the candidates questions related to the points discussed in Part 3, which broaden the topic and allow the candidates to discuss issues in more depth.

How to do the paper

Part 1

Listen carefully to the examiner's questions and to your partner's answers, as you might be asked the same or a similar question, or a completely different one.
Give full answers, adding relevant comments, reasons or examples.

Part 2

First compare the two pictures, pointing out similarities and differences.
Then move to the next task written above the photographs.

Part 3

First explore each of the issues suggested by the written prompts. Don't be afraid to give opinions and make comments, agreeing or disagreeing with your partner.
Then when reaching a decision, remember there are no right or wrong choices and you won't be given marks on your opinions but on the language you produce.

Part 4

Answer questions in depth and express your opinions clearly.
Involve your partner in the discussion.

Part 1 (2 minutes)

The examiner will ask you a few questions about yourself and what you think about different things. For example, the examiner might ask you about:

Every day life

- **Do you live in a house or in a flat? (Tell us about it.)**
- **What do you usually have for breakfast?**
- **What do you do like to do when you get home after a day at college / work?**
- **Do you like spending your free time with your family? (Why / Why not?)**

The future

- **Would you like to learn another language? (Why? / Why not?)**
- **Have you got any plans for next weekend?**
- **Is there a skill you would like to learn in the near future? (Why?)**
- **What type of work would you like to do in the future? (Why?)**

Free time

- **Do you like playing computer games in your free time? (Why? / Why not?)**
- **What is your favourite television programme? (Tell us about it.)**
- **How often do you go out with your friends? (Tell us what you do.)**
- **Is there something you enjoy doing on your own in your free time?**

Part 2 (4 minutes)

I'm going to give each of you two photographs. I'd like you to talk about your photographs on your own for about a minute, and also to answer a question about your partner's photographs.

(Candidate A), look at the photographs on page 169 which show **people studying**. I'd like you to compare the photographs, and say **why the people have chosen to study in these places**.

Thank you. *(Candidate B)*, **do you ever study in a library**?

Now, *(Candidate B)*, turn to the photographs on page 170. They show **people doing exercise**. I'd like you to compare the photographs, and say **how good these types of exercise might be for the people in the photos**.

Thank you. *(Candidate A)*, **do you like team sports?**

Part 3 (4 minutes)

Now I'd like you to talk about something together for about two minutes. Now look at page 171.

Here are some problems people may have to deal with when they are travelling on holiday, and a question for you to discuss. First you have some time to look at the task.

Now talk to each other about **how serious these problems might be when people go on holiday**.

Thank you. Now you have a minute to decide **which problem would be the most stressful**.

TIP STRIP

For the first part of the task you could say: Some of these situations are serious whilst others are easy to deal with. Running out of money would be a disaster. I don't think young people would miss their families, but some may miss the comforts of home. If there are disagreements with friends, that could ruin the whole trip, unless they discuss the problems.

For the second part: I think the most stressful situation would be if somebody is ill and needs a doctor.

Part 4 (4 minutes)

Use the following questions in order, as appropriate:

- **Have you ever had to deal with problems like these? How did you react?**

- **Do you like holidays which are full of activities? (Why / Why not?)**

- **Would you rather go on holiday with people of your own age? (Why?)**

- **How important is it to organise a trip in advance?**

- **Some people prefer short holidays to long ones. What do you think?**

- **How important is it for young people to see what life is like in other countries?**

Select any of the following prompts, as appropriate:

- **What do you think?**

- **Do you agree?**

- **And you?**

Thank you. That is the end of the test.

TIP STRIP

Possible answers are:

Q3: It's easier to travel with people your age as you're likely to agree about things. Going with your parents can be good as they often pay.

Q4: It depends on the type of person you are and if you're travelling alone or in a group. I think it's more fun not to plan.

GUIDANCE: READING AND USE OF ENGLISH

Testing focus

Part 1
In Part 1, you'll find a range of testing focuses. Most questions test your knowledge of vocabulary and how it is used. Questions may focus on:
- general vocabulary related to the topic of the text.
- the relationship between words, e.g. which preposition is used after a word, or whether it is followed by an infinitive or a gerund.
- knowledge of fixed expressions and collocations.
- your knowledge of linking words and phrases. This tests whether you've understood the meaning of the whole text.

Part 2
Part 2 mostly tests your knowledge of grammar and sentence structure. Questions can focus on:
- the relationship between words, e.g. which words go together to form a fixed expression or phrasal verb.
- sentence structure, e.g. to insert the correct relative pronoun.
- other grammatical words, for example quantifiers, articles, etc.
- linking words and phrases to test whether you have understood the meaning of the whole text.

Part 3
Part 3 tests whether you can create the correct form of the word to fit in the sentence. Questions may focus on:
- your knowledge of prefixes and suffixes.
- your grammatical knowledge, e.g. which form of the word is needed to complete the meaning in the sentence.
- common expressions and collocations.
- your knowledge of compound words.

Part 4
Part 4 tests your knowledge of both grammar and vocabulary. Questions always have two testing points, for example you may need to change the form of a word from the input sentence as well as creating a new sentence pattern.
- You're tested on your ability to express the same ideas using different grammatical forms and patterns, for example, by completing a sentence that starts with a different word.
- Questions may test your knowledge of fixed phrases and collocations by asking you to find the words that combine with those already in the target sentence.
- Your answers must be grammatically accurate.

Part 5
The questions in Part 5 all have the same multiple-choice format. Questions may focus on:
- Your detailed understanding of one section of the text.

- The writer's attitude or intended message.
- The use of particular vocabulary or expressions.
- The use of reference words.

Some questions focus on a phrase or sentence in the text, whilst others will ask you to interpret the meaning of a larger section of text. Look for clues in the questions to help you find the targeted piece of text. For example, 'In the third paragraph' is a clear indication of the piece of text you need to read; but it also tells you not to consider information and ideas from elsewhere in the text.

Part 6
Part 6 tests your ability to see the links between the different parts of a text and use these to put a jumbled text into the correct order. These links can be of different types and, often, more than one type of link helps you to answer the question. Look for:
- vocabulary links between the paragraphs, especially where an idea from one paragraph is developed in the next one. Don't expect to see the same word used, however. You should look for different words with a similar meaning.
- grammatical links between paragraphs, especially the use of pronouns and other words that refer to things that have already been mentioned.
- logical links of topic and focus. Look for where people, places or ideas are first introduced in the text. If these appear in an option, then that sentence must fit later in the text.

You're looking for links that work, but also looking for links that don't work. For example, if a paragraph in the options seems to fit a gap logically and contains the right sort of ideas and vocabulary, you need to check whether there are any references in the option that don't have a point of reference in the surrounding text.

Part 7
In Part 7, you're being tested on your ability to locate relevant parts of the text, or texts, and match them to the ideas in the prompt questions. Two types of reading skill are involved:
- the ability to read through a text, understand its organisation and locate the parts relevant to a particular prompt. This involves reading quickly to get a general idea of the text, without worrying about the meaning of every word or the exact point being made.
- the skill of careful reading to understand the precise meaning in both the prompt question and in the relevant part of the base text. The prompt question will report ideas from the text, but will not use the same vocabulary and ideas to do this.

Preparation tips

- Do as many practice tests as possible so that you know what is expected of you, and you feel confident going into the exam.
- Remember that the First exam aims to test real life skills. The reading that you do outside the classroom will help you.
- Keep a vocabulary notebook and use it to keep a record of useful vocabulary that you come across, arranged by topic.
- Try to learn words in chunks rather than in isolation. When you learn a new word, write down both the word, and the sentence it's used in.
- When you're doing practice tests, keep a note of questions you get wrong and attempt them again two weeks later.
- Write a verb on one side of a card, and its dependent preposition on the other. Test yourself on them. This will help with Parts 1 and 2.
- Choose a text in English and underline all the prepositions. Then decide which ones are part of set word patterns. This will help with Parts 1 and 2.

- Go through a reading text and write a list of all of the adjectives. Is there a noun in the same verb family? What about an adverb? This will help with Parts 3 and 4.
- To help with Part 5, read texts which express people's attitudes and opinions, such as interviews with famous people, and concentrate on understanding their opinions and feelings.
- Look at English-language news articles and note down the phrases used to link the paragraphs. This will help you with Part 6.
- Practise reading texts quickly all the way through to understand the gist. Read online articles and summarise the main ideas or opinions in them.

Part 1

For questions **1 – 8**, read the text below and decide which answer (**A**, **B**, **C** or **D**) best fits each gap. There is an example at the beginning (**0**).

In the exam, you mark your answers **on a separate answer sheet**.

Example:

| 0 | **A** known | **B** entitled | **C** referred | **D** called |

| 0 | A B C D |

TIP STRIP

Question 2: Which word used with 'for' makes a phrasal verb which means 'requires'?

Question 3: Only one of the words collocates with 'knowledge'.

Question 6: Only one of these words can be followed by the preposition 'from'.

Sudoku

Are you a fan of the popular logical puzzle that is **(0)** .... as Sudoku? In the early years of this century, this addictive Japanese brain-teaser became a common feature of newspaper puzzle pages the world over. Sudoku's great success **(1)** .... much to its simplicity. The game **(2)** .... for neither mathematical ability nor **(3)** .... knowledge and there are just a few sentences of straightforward instructions to read before you can play.

Western newspapers worked **(4)** .... at promoting the game. Without this, it's unlikely that it would have **(5)** .... off and become quite such a runaway success. The game also **(6)** .... from its Japanese name. This led may people to **(7)** .... it as a superior kind of puzzle compared to those usually found in newspapers.

When the popularity of Sudoku was at its peak, newspapers responded by introducing new logical puzzles, all with simple rules and Japanese names. For true Sudoku fans **(8)** .... , only the real thing will do.

1	**A** results	**B** thanks	**C** owes	**D** lends
2	**A** expects	**B** demands	**C** requests	**D** calls
3	**A** general	**B** normal	**C** usual	**D** ordinary
4	**A** tough	**B** hard	**C** strong	**D** heavy
5	**A** made	**B** taken	**C** given	**D** passed
6	**A** promoted	**B** improved	**C** benefitted	**D** increased
7	**A** believe	**B** regard	**C** think	**D** consider
8	**A** however	**B** although	**C** therefore	**D** despite

Part 2

For questions **9 – 16**, read the text below and think of the word which best fits each gap. Use only **one** word in each gap. There is an example at the beginning (**0**).

In the exam, you write your answers **IN CAPITAL LETTERS on a separate answer sheet**.

Example: | **0** | W | E | R | E | | | | | | | | | | | | | | | | |

The Birth of *YouTube*

In 2005, Chad Hurley and Steve Chen, two software designers from Silicon Valley in California, **(0)** .... invited to a dinner party. The conversation turned to home videos and people started complaining about **(9)** .... difficult it was to share these online. That was when Chad and Steve came up **(10)** .... the idea for *YouTube*. They formed a company, borrowed some money and **(11)** .... themselves up in business.

It turned out that millions of people already had short home-video clips they thought it **(12)** .... be fun to share, and the site soon contained more **(13)** .... a million clips. Contributors mostly heard about the site through word of mouth, and clips were mostly made by amateurs.

So why was *YouTube* such an immediate success? It was discovered that, **(14)** .... average, users were spending fifteen minutes on the site during each visit, **(15)** .... was enough time to view several short funny clips. In **(16)** .... words, they were using *YouTube* to give them a short break from work or study.

TIP STRIP

Question 10: You need a preposition to complete a multi-word verb

Question 11: You need a verb that is part of a phrasal verb.

Question 12: You need a modal verb here.

For questions **17 – 24**, read the text below. Use the word given in capitals at the end of some of the lines to form a word that fits in the gap **in the same line**. There is an example at the beginning (**0**).

In the exam, you write your answers **IN CAPITAL LETTERS on a separate answer sheet**.

Example:

| 0 | I | N | C | R | E | A | S | I | N | G | | | | | | | | |

Putting the fun back into driving

With the **(0)** .... numbers of cars on the roads nowadays, few people seem to get the chance to go out driving purely for **(17)** .... Although the number of vehicles and drivers has risen, there has been relatively little **(18)** .... in the road network. The result is greater emphasis on road **(19)** .... , which has meant the **(20)** .... of tougher driving regulations. Motorists who enjoy going fast, for example, may be more likely to end up with a fine for speeding.

INCREASE

PLEASE

GROW

SAFE

INTRODUCE

One answer is something called a track day, an event where people can drive their own cars around a racing circuit, and explore the limits of their **(21)** .... without endangering other road users. Track days tend to be **(22)** .... days out rather than competitive events, and people go for the sheer enjoyment of driving. Track days are growing in **(23)** .... as drivers only have to follow a few basic rules and a **(24)** .... of vehicles and age groups is welcome.

PERFORM

FORMAL

POPULAR

VARY

For questions **25 – 30**, complete the second sentence so that it has a similar meaning to the first sentence, using the word given. **Do not change the word given.** You must use between **two** and **five** words, including the word given. Here is an example (**0**).

Example:

0   What type of music do you like best?

FAVOURITE

What .... type of music?

The gap can be filled with the words 'is your favourite', so you write:

Example:	0	*IS YOUR FAVOURITE*

In the exam, you write only the missing words **IN CAPITAL LETTERS on a separate answer sheet.**

TIP STRIP

Question 25: How do you make a comparison using 'as'?

Question 26: You need to use reported speech here.

Question 28: You're looking for a phrase that means 'participate'

25   I expected ice-skating to be more difficult than it actually was.

NOT

Ice-skating .... as I'd expected.

26   'Leon, I think you should tell your mother the truth,' said Maite.

ADVISED

Maite .... his mother the truth.

27   Not many people went to see that live concert in the park.

NUMBER

Only .... went to see that live concert in the park.

28   How many competitors went in for the race?

PART

How many competitors .... the race?

29   You can borrow my new bicycle, but you must be careful with it.

LONG

You can borrow my new bicycle .... careful with it.

30   Melanie regretted choosing such an expensive jacket.

WISHED

Melanie .... a less expensive jacket.

Part 5

You are going to read an extract from a novel. For questions **31 – 36**, choose the answer (**A**, **B**, **C** or **D**) which you think fits best according to the text.

In the exam, you mark your answers **on a separate answer sheet**.

There was a book with bed and breakfast places in it amongst the guidebooks and maps on the back seat of my aunt's car and we found somewhere to stay in there. It was a big, old farmhouse down the end of a track. There were three cows in the nearest field, sheep up on a ridge, hens in the yard, a few sheds and barns standing around and a rosy-cheeked farmer's wife. After a day driving round, I was really impressed with the place initially, thinking we'd finally found the true countryside. Now my aunt could write whatever she was supposed to write about it, and we could both relax and go home.

But when I suggested that, she just said she wasn't expected to write about accommodation. Then, when we got talking to the woman, the place wasn't quite what it seemed anyway. The only field that went with the farmhouse was the one beside the track, with the cows in it, the rest belonged to a farm over the hill. The barns were rented to another farmer and the woman came from the city and was married to a travelling salesman. From close to, you could see the colour in her cheeks came out of a jar marked 'blusher'. The hens were hers, though. She'd been a professional bed and breakfast lady for three years, she said, and this was the worst season ever, and yes we could have separate rooms, two of each if we liked.

Perhaps she and her husband spent all their money on winter holidays, or perhaps they just didn't have any, but they certainly didn't spend a lot on the house. The bedrooms were huge but they hardly had any furniture in them – just a double bed in each, one of those wardrobes with hangers on one side and shelves down the other, and a wooden chair. There was a dangling light cord over each bed, which worked the centre light, but no bedside lamp.

I could tell that my aunt wasn't knocked out by it because she whispered to me, 'All very clean, isn't it?' which is what mum says about a place when she can't find anything else good. 'Well there isn't much to get dirty,' I whispered back. But the woman, Mrs Vosper, obviously assumed we'd stay, so we did. She asked if we were on holiday, and I listened with interest to my aunt's answer. I don't think I really understood at that point what she was doing, and it had got a bit late to ask her myself. I was supposed to know. But all she said was: 'Touring around, taking a bit of a break.' So that didn't help me much.

When I got into bed, I didn't feel very sleepy. My aunt had given me a copy of the magazine she was working for, so I had a look at that. It was called Holiday UK and the cover had 'London' printed across one corner and a colour picture of horses in a park. There was a great long article by my aunt inside, which went on for about six pages, with lots of photographs, each with her name up the side of it. But there were also adverts for hotels and restaurants and shops, along with a couple of pages listing places to eat, theatres, cinemas, that sort of stuff. Also it was clear that you didn't have to pay for it, so I realised it couldn't be up to much. Still I knew they must somehow have enough money to pay her, or they couldn't send her rushing around the countryside like this.

31 What did the writer think of the farmhouse when she first saw it?

   A   It was better than the description in the guidebook.

   B   It lived up to her expectations of the countryside.

   C   It was similar to one her aunt had written about.

   D   It reminded her of her own house at home.

32 What do we discover about the farm in the second paragraph?

   A   It wasn't as large as it seemed.

   B   None of the animals belonged to it.

   C   The owner lived in another part of the country.

   D   The bed and breakfast business was doing well.

33 What disappointed the writer about the accommodation offered at the farm?

   A   the lack of space to hang clothes

   B   the fact that it needed cleaning

   C   the limited amount of furniture

   D   the size of the rooms

34 When Mrs Vosper asked if they were on holiday, the writer felt

   A   embarrassed by her aunt's reply.

   B   unsure why her aunt had really come.

   C   too tired to take in what was being said.

   D   worried that she might be asked something next.

35 The word 'it' in line **27** refers to

   A   a page in the magazine.

   B   an article in the magazine.

   C   a photograph in the magazine.

   D   an advertisement in the magazine.

36 The writer was unimpressed by the magazine because

   A   it didn't contain any interesting stories.

   B   it provided only factual information.

   C   it seemed to be all about London.

   D   it was given away free to people.

TIP STRIP

Question 31: The answer is in the first paragraph. Look for a word that matches 'first' in the question.

Question 34: Find Mrs Vosper's name in the extract. The answer comes after this.

Question 36: Most of the final paragraph describes the magazine. Look for an expression the writer uses to give her opinion of it.

Part 6

You are going to read an extract from an article about a trip to study the bottlenose whale. Six sentences have been removed from the article. Choose from the sentences **A – G** the one which fits each gap (**37 – 42**). There is one extra sentence you do not need to use.

In the exam, you mark your answers **on a separate answer sheet**.

Bottlenose whales: deep-sea divers of the North Atlantic

Douglas Chadwick joined the crew of the research boat the 'Balaena'

I have joined the crew of the *Balaena*, a fifteen-metre research boat, and we're now a few kilometres off the east coast of Canada, sailing over what seafarers call the Gully. Gully means 'narrow channel', but this is more like a drowned Grand Canyon, about ten kilometres across and, in places, over a kilometre straight down to the bottom of the sea. The Gully, with its abundant fish, is home to a dozen species of cetaceans.

We've come in search of northern bottlenose whales. Hal Whitehead, a whale expert, and his crew are here to study the behaviour of these enigmatic creatures. I'm hoping to see at least one today, but I'm prepared to be disappointed. I've been told that, as a rule, the first things you see are spouts, the typical jets of water coming out of the animals' heads, which are visible from a distance. **37**

Already some three-metres long at birth, northern bottlenoses continue to grow in size until the age of twenty, when they may reach ten metres. Adults weigh between five and seven tons, roughly the same as African elephants. **38** 'These are probably among the most intelligent animals on the entire planet, and we hardly know a thing about them,' says Hal Whitehead.

It's very quiet and all we can hear is the creak of the ship's masts as it sways. Suddenly, breaths like great sighs sound through the fog. **39** The smallest one swims for the boat and a larger companion cuts it off. Then they rejoin the others to float like swollen logs a short distance away.

I can see them well. They have small fins but big, domed heads with imposing foreheads above narrow, protruding jaws. Their heads are two-thirds out of the water now, all pointing our way. **40** We are being studied by northern bottlenose whales, which is only fair, since that is what we came to do to them.

If the bottlenoses don't swim too fast, we can keep up and observe them. Their movements are accompanied by grunts, whistles and cheers made by the blowholes. Every so often, one repeatedly lifts its tail to give the water a resounding slap. This display may function as yet another way to be heard. **41**

The biggest question is what goes on when these animals aren't on the surface, which is most of the time. To find out, the researchers attached a time-depth recorder (TDR) to one whale's skin. The TDR stayed on four-and-a-half hours and surfaced with the first solid data ever obtained about a bottlenose in its submarine kingdom. **42** This revelation seems to prove Hal Whitehead's theory that the world's deepest diver is the bottlenose whale – or maybe one of the many other related species of beaked whales, which are yet to be studied.

A When you come closer, though, you may find that they have submerged on a long dive, presumably in search of food.

B On one of its dives, the bottlenose had reached a depth of nine-hundred metres.

C These animals aren't just watching us, they are scanning us with rapid clicking noises just above the range of human hearing.

D Whale hunting reduced the population by at least seventy per cent, and the species remains depleted today.

E The same holds for leaping skyward and making a huge splash, though they may do this just for fun.

F Beyond these basic facts, little is known about the lives of northern bottlenoses.

G These strange noises come from four creatures, twenty to thirty feet long, which have risen from the depths.

TIP STRIP

Question 37: Look for a word in the options which also talks about 'distance'.

Question 39: Which option picks up on the idea of 'sounds' before the gap?

Question 42: Find the sentence that links 'the first solid data' before the gap with 'This revelation' after gap

Part 7

You are going to read a magazine article about four women who are referees or umpires in different sports. For questions **43 – 52**, choose from the graduates (**A – D**). The women may be chosen more than once.

In the exam, you mark your answers **on a separate answer sheet**.

Which woman …

remembers feeling confident when she started doing the work? | 43

mentions a personal quality that's appreciated by male players? | 44

gives an example of the way that standards are maintained in the job? | 45

mentions the need to communicate with a colleague during matches? | 46

says people feel more positive about her after seeing her in action? | 47

intends to do something so that other women can reach her position? | 48

feels that people are generally unaware of the demands of her role? | 49

remembers her surprise at hearing she'd been accepted in the role? | 50

mentions her good relations with other sports professionals? | 51

seems to behaves differently when she's actually doing the job? | 52

TIP STRIP

Question 43: A and D both talk about starting out in their role – but which of them felt confident at that time?

Question 44: Three of the women mention working with men, but which one talks about something they like about her?

Question 50: Look for an expression that means 'surprised' to find the answer.

What's it like to be a female referee or umpire in a major sport?

A Bentla D'Couth: Football referee

When you first meet Bentla D'Couth, who was India's first ever female football referee, appearances can be deceptive. She's soft-spoken and appears shy and unassuming, in sharp contrast to how she is on the field, where she comes across as loud and aggressive. Bentla was always interested in football, but it was only at the age of eighteen that she learnt of the existence of women's football. 'In my first refereeing job, I made sure I was on top of every detail of the game so that I couldn't make a wrong decision,' she says. 'It doesn't happen now, but I guess in those days some people did have that 'what would she know about football?' attitude. But once they saw me on the field, refereeing a match, they soon changed their tune. I can't say that I've had any bad experiences so far.' Bentla knows she has to improve on her positioning, though. 'Men play very fast, so it can be tough keeping up with that pace.'

B Ria Cortesio: Baseball umpire

Ria Cortesio, a native of Davenport, Iowa, is one of the few women umpires in professional baseball in the USA. By doing TV talk shows and other public appearances, she's hoping to open doors so that others can follow in her footsteps. Asked what drove her as a young person to take on the role, which she refers to as 'the challenge', she says: 'I don't think that it's widely appreciated what it means to work at professional games day in, day out, always on the road,' she says. 'It's you against the world during the season. It really doesn't make any difference being a woman on the field – or even off the field, and the one group of people I haven't had a single problem with are the male players, coaches or managers. If anything, they tend to be even more respectful to me than they'd usually be.'

C Gill Clarke: Hockey umpire

'I've just umpired at my third Olympics, which was quite an achievement for a British woman,' explains Gill Clarke. An umpire's performance is assessed in all international matches, and they have to score a minimum 8 out of 10 every time to keep their position. 'Factors included in the assessment are such things as signalling clearly to the other umpire on the pitch, as well as fitness and controlling the game,' says Clarke. She arrived at the Olympics early to get over the stresses and strains of the flight, ready for the pressures of the two weeks of the hockey competition. 'Increasingly, there's more at stake,' she says, 'it's big money for the players and the coaches, but for umpires only personal satisfaction at a job well done.'

D Grace Gavin: Rugby referee

When Grace Gavin heard that her application to become a rugby referee had been accepted, she was in a taxi. 'I was completely taken aback, and quite nervous at the prospect,' she recalls. Grace combines her refereeing with a full-time job. 'I strongly believe that if we referee world-class athletes, we must train like world-class athletes. This is difficult to manage when you also have work commitments. My boss was happy when I retired from playing because the black eyes that I sported some Monday mornings weren't going down well with clients.' Early in her refereeing career, somebody told Grace that she'd always be handicapped by the perception that she wasn't fast enough to referee men's rugby. 'I've worked constantly to defeat this perception,' she says. 'Surprisingly, many players like having me as a ref because they can hear my voice. They can pick it out more easily than they could a male voice in the heat of the match.

GUIDANCE: WRITING

Testing focus

Both parts carry equal marks. Spelling and punctuation, the right length, paragraphing and legible handwriting are taken into account in both parts of the test.

Part 1

- **content:** Have you included the three points required, including one of your own? Is the content of your piece relevant, i.e. are all the points clearly connected with the task?
- **organisation:** Have you organised your essay so that the different paragraphs and sentences are connected logically? Have you used a range of words and phrases to link sentences and paragraphs (not just basic linking words such as 'but')?
- **language:** Have you used a range of language? Have you used varied vocabulary, including some less common lexis? Have you used some complex structures, using linking words and different tenses? Is the grammar and vocabulary correct?
- **communicative achievement:** Is the style you have used appropriately formal? Have you communicated your ideas (both simple and complex) in an effective way, holding the reader's attention? Would the reader of your essay understand all your arguments?

Part 2

- **content:** Have you included all the information required in the task? Is the content of your piece relevant, i.e. are all the points clearly connected with the task?
- organisation: Have you organised your piece in clear paragraphs? Have you used a range of words and phrases to link paragraphs and sentences (not just basic linking words such as 'but')?
- **language:** Have you used a range of language? Have you used varied vocabulary, including some less common lexis? Have you used some complex structures, using linking words and different tenses? Is the grammar and vocabulary correct?
- **communicative achievement:** Have you used the correct format (e.g. article) and the correct style (e.g. semi-formal) for the task? (Though there is no compulsory format for the different task types, the use of appropriate features of presentation, such as headings for reports, will be given credit.) Would the reader be fully informed and find your piece of writing interesting?

Preparation tips

Look at good examples and learn from them. Use the Writing Bank on pages 162–168, which also gives you useful language you can use. Look at the sample answers in the multiROM? to see what may win or lose you marks.

Part 1

- Practise writing the essay in the time allowed and keeping to the required number of words.
- Work with a partner to discuss content and organisation and to correct each other's language errors.
- Practise developing an argument for or against an idea, giving your opinions and backing them up with a few reasons.

Part 2

- Work on improving your wealth of vocabulary by reading as widely as possible and noting down words and expressions you might want to use.
- Look at examples of articles, reviews, reports and letters in English-language newspapers and magazines. How are they organised? What makes them interesting to read?

Part I

You **must** answer this question. Write your answer in **140 – 190** words in an appropriate style.

1   In your English class you have been discussing the importance of having good friends. Now your English teacher has asked you to write an essay.

Write an essay using **all** the notes and giving reasons for your point of view.

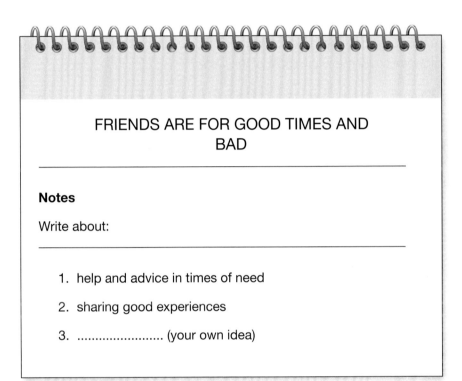

FRIENDS ARE FOR GOOD TIMES AND BAD

Notes

Write about:

1. help and advice in times of need

2. sharing good experiences

3. .... (your own idea)

Write your **essay**.

Part 2

Write an answer to **one** of the questions **2 – 4** in this part. Write your answer in **140 – 190** words in an appropriate style.

___

2   Your English friend is coming to visit you next month and this is part of an email he has sent you.

> I'm looking forward to this trip, but you know me, I like to plan everything! I'd like to go and see as much music as possible, without spending too much, and also visit some museums. Have you had any thoughts about how we could make the most of the week?
>
> Simon

Write your **email**.

3   You recently saw this notice in the local newspaper.

> ### Write a review of a TV nature programme and win a camera!
> Include information about the content of the programme and the locations where it was filmed, and say whether you think people of all ages would enjoy it.

Write your **review.**

4   You recently saw this announcement in an online magazine for English language students.

> # Are you good at writing?
> Write an article for us on the topic below and you could see it published here soon!
>
> **A person I was very pleased to meet**
>
> Tell us how you met this person, why he or she became so important to you, and what has happened to your relationship since then.

Write your **article**.

GUIDANCE: LISTENING

Testing focus

Part 1

There is a range of testing focuses in Part 1 questions.

- Some questions focus on a detailed understanding of parts of the text, or on the use of particular vocabulary or expressions.
- Some questions test your understanding of the text as a whole, or of the speakers' attitudes, feelings or opinions.

Part 2

Part 2 tests your ability to locate, understand and record specific information from the recording.

- This task does not test grammar, so you don't have to change the form of the words you hear. However, you should check the grammar of the sentence to check if the word you have heard is, for example, singular or plural.
- Only write the word or words that are needed to complete the sentence. There are no marks for extra information. If you write too much, you risk losing the mark by not creating a good sentence.

Part 3

Each question matches one of the speakers. The five speakers are talking about the same topic and will probably use the same vocabulary and discuss the same ideas. Listen to understand the meaning of what

each speaker says – not just the words and expressions they use. Listen to the instructions to know what you're listening for, for example is it the speaker's opinion or how the speaker felt about something, or are you listening for the speaker's main point.

- Some questions focus on a phrase or sentence in the recording.
- Some questions ask you to understand the gist of what a speaker is saying.

Part 4

Part 4 tests a detailed understanding of the speakers' feelings, attitudes and opinions. There is a range of testing focuses:

- Some questions focus on a phrase or sentence in the recording.
- Some questions ask you to understand the gist of what the main speaker is saying.

Each question relates to a specific section of the recording and there is a range of testing focuses. The answer to each question usually comes from one long turn from the main speaker, usually in answer to a question from an interviewer. Listen to the interviewer's questions and see how this relates to the questions in the task.

Preparations tip

- Remember that the Cambridge First exam aims to test real life skills, so any listening practice you do is likely to improve your general listening skills.
- When you're doing practice tests, think about different ways in which the same idea can be expressed, for example 'What's the price?' and 'How much does it cost?' are different ways of saying the same thing. The questions in the listening are not going to include exactly the same words that you hear in the recording, so think about the meaning of what people are saying.

- Practise using the sample answer sheets so that you know how to fill them in on the day of the exam. Make sure you always put the correct answer next to each number.
- Search online for English language radio programmes, podcasts and video clips on subjects that interest you. Don't expect to understand every word, but use your knowledge of the topic to understand the gist of what is being said. Note down the key ideas as you listen.

Part 1

You will hear people talking in eight different situations. For questions **1 – 8**, choose the best answer (**A**, **B** or **C**).

1   You hear a man talking about a ceramics course he attended.
    What aspect of the course did he find unsatisfactory?
    A   the level of support from the staff
    B   the quality of the materials
    C   the cost for students

2   On a radio programme, you hear some information about a future guest.
    What will he be talking about?
    A   organising a mountain holiday.
    B   learning mountain climbing skills.
    C   buying mountaineering equipment.

3   You hear part of a talk about how to look fit and healthy.
    What is the speaker's advice?
    A   check your weight regularly
    B   build up your muscles
    C   avoid certain foods

4   You overhear two college students talking about applying for a weekend job.
    What do they agree about?
    A   It would be an enjoyable thing to do.
    B   It would be useful experience for the future.
    C   It would help them with their college expenses.

5   You hear two friends talking about transport.
    The woman has decided to use a bike instead of a car because
    A   she hopes the exercise will improve her health.
    B   she is concerned about the environment.
    C   she can no longer afford the cost.

6   You hear a woman talking about a sport.
    What is she doing?
    A   explaining something to us
    B   warning us about something
    C   recommending something to us

7   You hear a weather forecast on the radio.
    How will the weather change tomorrow?
    A   It will get colder.
    B   It will get sunnier.
    C   It will get windier.

8   You hear a news report about a theatre.
    What does the reporter say about it?
    A   It is offering an impressive programme.
    B   It will be closed down in the near future.
    C   It has received a grant for improvements.

You will hear a student giving a presentation on the subject of the Loch Ness Monster. For questions **9 – 18**, complete the sentences with a word or short phrase.

The Loch Ness Monster

The head of the Loch Ness Monster has been compared to that of a

(9) ....

The first published photographic image of the monster is known as the

(10) .... picture.

People argued that a picture taken in 1960 actually showed a

(11) .... but experts proved them wrong.

Tim Dinsdale realised that most monster sightings occurred on days when the weather was

(12) ....

Most eyewitnesses say that they have no interest in getting

(13) .... when they report sightings.

In 1968, an underwater investigation used sonar equipment instead of

(14) .... to try and find the monster.

An attempt to find the monster using a **(15)** ....

failed in 1969 because the water was so dirty.

The idea of using a group of **(16)** ....

to help with the search proved too complicated.

Dr Rines' underwater picture of 1972 seemed to show the

(17) .... of a large sea animal.

The aim of the latest research project is to study all the

(18) ....

and .... living in Loch Ness.

TIP STRIP

Question 12: Be careful – different types of weather are mentioned. Listen for when it's easiest to see the monster.

Question 13: Listen for a similar way of expressing the idea 'have no interest in'.

Question 18: You are listening for two words here that can be connected by the word 'and'

Part 3

You will hear five short extracts in which people are talking about a concert they went to. For questions **19 – 23**, choose from the list (**A – H**) the opinion each speaker expresses. There are three extra letters which you do not need to use.

A   The performers got a better reception than they deserved.

B   These musicians are at their best in live performances.

Speaker 1 [   ] **19**

C   It improved after a disappointing beginning.

Speaker 2 [   ] **20**

D   I enjoyed the band's choice of material.

Speaker 3 [   ] **21**

E   I expected it to go on for longer than it did.

Speaker 4 [   ] **22**

F   I'd like to have seen more bands for the price I paid.

Speaker 5 [   ] **23**

G   I was annoyed by the behaviour of some band members.

H   I was pleased the event was raising money for a good cause.

You will hear an interview with a man called Patrick Shaw who works as a pilot for a company which organises hot-air balloon trips. For questions **24 – 30**, choose the best answer (**A**, **B** or **C**).

24 According to Patrick, what worries people most when they take a balloon trip?

    A   how far the wind will take them

    B   whether they will hit some obstacle

    C   what the experience of landing will be like

25 Why does Patrick recommend joining the ground crew?

    A   It's the best way of learning about balloons.

    B   It provides some experience of flying a balloon.

    C   It can be a fun way of earning extra income.

26 What makes the job of the ground crew particularly difficult?

    A   poor communication with the pilot

    B   unpredictable weather conditions

    C   the nervousness of the passengers

27 Patrick says that all members of the ground crew must

    A   be physically strong.

    B   have good social skills.

    C   know their area well.

28 Patrick finds it unsatisfactory when new crew members

    A   fail to cooperate with each other.

    B   distract him with unnecessary questions.

    C   don't accept the way things should be done.

29 What does Patrick say about balloon competitions?

    A   It is often difficult to determine who has won.

    B   The finishing target area is often unmarked.

    C   Some competitors are requesting clearer rules.

30 Patrick thinks his particular skills as a pilot result from

    A   the way in which he was trained.

    B   the fact that he's adventurous by nature.

    C   the amount of experience he has.

TIP STRIP

Question 24: Listen for a word with a similar meaning to 'worries'. What is it referring to?

Question 26: Patrick mentions several difficulties, but which one is the most serious?

Question 28: Be careful, you're listening for something which Patrick doesn't like.

GUIDANCE: SPEAKING

Testing focus

Candidates will be assessed on the following:
- grammar and vocabulary
- discourse management
- pronunciation
- interactive communication
- global achievement

Part 1

In this part, candidates have to show that they are able to use everyday social and interactional language. Examiners will encourage the use of natural language and discourage prepared speeches. Students will need to speak clearly and show an ability to use good basic grammar and a good range of vocabulary.

Part 2

This part tests the candidates' ability to speak for 1 minute without the examiner's support. candidates have to be able to produce a long stretch of language which fulfils the task they have been given. They have to organise their ideas in such a way as to make it easy for the listener to understand. This will require the use of some complex language forms, different tenses, linking words, etc.

Part 3

This part tests the candidates' ability to take part in a discussion by initiating, responding to their partner's comments, and inviting their partner's opinions. candidates will be assessed on their ability to express, justify and evaluate different opinions and on their use of the language of collaboration and negotiation. There is no right or wrong answer to this task and candidates won't be penalised if they fail to reach a decision.

Part 4

This part tests the candidates' ability to engage in a discussion and to deal with issues in more depth than in earlier parts of the test. candidates are expected to use a range of grammar and vocabulary when expressing ideas and opinions. They will be assessed on their use of language, not on the opinions they express.

Preparation tips

- **General:** Make sure you are familiar with the structure of the test: what you are expected to do in each part, what the examiner will say, what materials you will be given, how long each part lasts.
- Practise paraphrasing, i.e., expressing the same idea in different ways. This will be useful if you cannot remember a word or expression.
- **For Part 1**, practise talking about yourself with other students, on a range of different topics. Choose a topic, e.g. work, and ask each other a variety of questions.

- **For Part 2**, practise talking for a minute on a topic, with a classmate timing you. Think of how you want to organise your extended turn, and note down linking words you may want to use.
- **For Part 3**, practise talking about the content of each of the five written prompts as fully as possible.
- **For Part 4**, practise asking each other for your opinions on current events. When answering a question, always expand on your views.

Part 1 (2 minutes)

The examiner will ask you a few questions about yourself and what you think about different things. For example, the examiner might ask you about:

Education

- Do you use the internet when you study? (Why? / Why not?)
- Which musical instrument would you like to learn to play? (Why?)
- Which school / college subject did you find most difficult? (Why?)
- Do you prefer to study alone or with friends? (Why?)

TIP STRIP

Education

Question 1: Your answer can be 'yes' or 'no', but don't forget to add an explanation. You may want to say that you use it when you need information for an essay, or to find the answer to a difficult question. You may want to say that you prefer to go to the library or ask teachers or friends for information.

Question 3: Choose a subject and mention the reasons for finding it difficult. You could say English grammar is hard, and that you find verbs particularly difficult.

Health and fitness

- Is it important to take exercise every day? (Why? / Why not?)
- Is there a sport you like watching? (Tell us about it.)
- Do you think it's important to avoid unhealthy food? (Why? / Why not?)
- Do you like taking part in sports competitions? (Why? / Why not?)

TIP STRIP

Health and fitness

Question 1: If your answer is 'yes', you can say how it improves your health and how you're happier if you're physically active. If you answer is 'no', you could argue that walking to and from school is also good exercise.

Question 4: If you never take part in sports competitions, don't be afraid to say so but give your reasons. You could say you aren't the sporty type, or that you've never been any good at sport. You could say that you prefer activities such as hill walking, without the pressure of competition.

Family and home

- What activities do you like to do with your family? (Why?)
- Is it better to be part of a large family or a small family? (Why?)
- Do you prefer to spend your free time with your family or with friends? (Why?)
- Which member of your family do you get on best with? (Why?)

TIP STRIP

Family and home

Question 2: If you have never thought about this before, don't worry. You could mention some advantages of having a small family (for example, having all your parents' attention) and some advantages of having a large family (for example, having brothers and sisters to share things with).

Question 4: Choose a member of your family and say why you get on well together. You may want to say you have similar interests or that you're able to discuss your problems.

Part 2 (4 minutes)

I'm going to give each of you two photographs. I'd like you to talk about your photographs on your own for about a minute, and also to answer a question about your partner's photographs.

(Candidate A), it's your turn first. Look at the photographs on page 172. They show **people on holiday**. I'd like you to compare the photographs, and say **what type of person would choose these holidays**.

Thank you. *(Candidate B)*, **do you like beach holidays**?

Now *(Candidate B)*, look at your photogrpahs on page 173. They **show people waiting**. I'd like you to compare the photographs, and say **how the people may be feeling**.

Thank you. *(Candidate A)*, **do you mind having to wait sometimes**?

TIP STRIP

Candidate A: You could compare the crowds enjoying the beach and the group touring the city. You could refer to sunbathing, sandy beaches, enjoying water sports, being in a crowd, sharing the beach with lots of people, learning about the history of a town, people enjoying travelling in a group.

Candidate B: You could compare the excitement of the girls waiting at an airport with the boredom of most people waiting to go into the restaurant. You could refer to the long queues, to the people looking forward to a fun holiday and to spending time with friends.

Part 3 (4 minutes)

Now I'd like you to talk about something together for about two minutes.

A group of college students is organising a concert where local bands will play. Here are some jobs that need doing and a question for you to discuss. First you have some time to look at the task on page 174.

Now talk to each other about **how easy or difficult it might be for students to do these jobs**.

Now you have a minute to decide **which job would be the most challenging for the students**.

TIP STRIP

For the first part of the task you could say:
I think some of these jobs would be very hard if the students don't have any previous experience. For example, interviewing the musicians might seem easy, but you need to ask interesting questions. The same is true about writing a review. Introducing the bands is easy as long as you have a good voice and a good sound system.

For the second part:
I think the most challenging job is preparing the stage and the sound system because you need to have some expert knowledge. They might need the help of a specialist for this.

Part 4 (4 minutes)

Use the following questions in order, as appropriate:

- **Is it useful for students to get experience in organising events like this? (Why / Why not)?**
- **Why do people enjoy going to live concerts?**
- **Have you ever given a live performance? Tell us about it.**
- **Is it easier to learn new skills in a group or on your own? (Why / Why not)?**
- **What type of activity is good for relaxing after college / work?**
- **Do you think it's true that some people are better at organizing things than others? (Why / Why not)?**

Thank you. That is the end of the test.

Select any of the following prompts, as appropriate:

- **What do you think?**
- **Do you agree?**
- **And you?**

TIP STRIP

Question 1: Possible answers include: It's very useful for different reasons: they can learn how to do specific jobs, but they can also see how events like concerts are organised and why it's important to work as a team.

Question 5: Possible answers include: Some people find that watching an entertaining television programme helps them to relax, whilst others prefer to listen to music or to have a chat with friends. The most important thing is to forget all about work or college for a while.

Question 6: Possible answers include: I think it depends on how much experience they've had. Sometimes you don't know what you're good at until you try. But, yes, some people are more organised than others – and that's good, because it'd be boring if everybody was the same.

TEST 3

Part 1

For questions **1 – 8**, read the text below and decide which answer (**A**, **B**, **C** or **D**) best fits each gap. There is an example at the beginning (**0**).

In the exam, you mark your answers **on a separate answer sheet**.

Example:

0   **A** founded   **B** invented   **C** originated   **D** dicovered

0	A	B	C	D
	▬	▭	▭	▭

Boots for Africa

Sheffield Football Club was **(0)** .... over one-hundred-and-fifty years ago, and is the oldest in the world. Recently, the club has **(1)** .... forces with the world's largest express transportation company, *FedEx Express*, in a charitable scheme **(2)** .... as *Boots for Africa*. The **(3)** .... of the scheme is to send more than two thousand pairs of used football boots to young people living in remote rural areas in Africa, who are **(4)** .... in taking up the sport and setting up local teams.

People in Sheffield are being asked to donate any football boots, astro boots or football trainers of any size to the scheme. All the boots donated must be in good **(5)** .... , complete with laces and studs. Local businesses and schools can receive a special 'group donation pack'. This pack **(6)** .... posters and leaflets, which can be used to publicise the scheme, plus collection bags to encourage people to **(7)** .... a donation. The club's website has **(8)** .... information about the scheme.

1	**A** tied	**B** added	**C** joined	**D** linked
2	**A** named	**B** known	**C** called	**D** titled
3	**A** ambition	**B** motive	**C** reason	**D** aim
4	**A** interested	**B** curious	**C** keen	**D** attracted
5	**A** fitness	**B** state	**C** condition	**D** form
6	**A** contains	**B** combines	**C** composes	**D** consists
7	**A** put	**B** do	**C** hand	**D** make
8	**A** greater	**B** further	**C** wider	**D** larger

For questions **9 – 16**, read the text below and think of the word which best fits each gap. Use only **one** word in each gap. There is an example at the beginning (**0**).

In the exam, you write your answers **IN CAPITAL LETTERS on a separate answer sheet**.

Example: | **0** | M | O | S | T | | | | | | | | | | | | | | | |

An influential cook

Delia Smith is one of the **(0)** .... widely respected cookery writers in Britain. She made regular appearances in television cookery programmes **(9)** .... over forty years, and more than ten million copies of her cookery books have **(10)** .... sold.

Delia always says that her real skill is communication **(11)** .... than cooking. Indeed she had no formal cookery training **(12)** .... she began writing on the subject as a journalist on a daily newspaper. Delia writes simple step-by-step recipes **(13)** .... even inexperienced cooks can follow. What's **(14)** .... her recipes are tried and tested, Delia has made them successfully **(15)** .... least twenty times before they appear on television or in one of her books.

Because people trust Delia's recipes, they tend to take her advice **(16)** .... large numbers. For example, sales of cranberries increased by thirty per cent after Delia included the little red berries in a recipe for roast duck. In supermarkets across the country, shoppers were demanding cranberries, but unfortunately there were none left to buy.

For questions **17 – 24**, read the text below. Use the word given in capitals at the end of some of the lines to form a word that fits in the gap **in the same line**. There is an example at the beginning (**0**).

In the exam, you write your answers **IN CAPITAL LETTERS on a separate answer sheet**.

Example: | **0** | S | P | E | C | T | A | C | U | L | A | R | | | | | | | |

Young artists on display

The road to Elgol on the Isle of Skye provides one of the most
(**0**) .... and beautiful journeys in Scotland. It was an especially **SPECTACLE**
clear and lovely day when I travelled there to see an (**17**) .... of **EXHIBIT**
paintings by local primary school children.

The (**18**) .... designed school overlooks the sea, just next to the **TRADITION**
little harbour from which fishermen and boatloads of (**19**) .... set **TOUR**
out. From the playground the children have (**20**) .... views of the **WONDER**
nearby Cuillin Mountains and the gigantic cliffs along the seashore.

The children take a great (**21**) .... in their local environment and **PROUD**
this is evident in their art work. There were some very fine landscapes
on display, and several of the young artists demonstrated a keen
interest in either the mountains or the sea.

Each child had chosen a (**22**) .... piece to be framed, and these **FAVOUR**
made a very (**23**) .... display. Not surprisingly, all the framed **EFFECT**
paintings were soon bought by (**24**) .... visitors to the school. **ENTHUSIAST**

Part 4

For questions **25 – 30**, complete the second sentence so that it has a similar meaning to the first sentence, using the word given. **Do not change the word given.** You must use between **two** and **five** words, including the word given. Here is an example (**0**).

Example:

0 What type of music do you like best?

FAVOURITE

What .... type of music?

The gap can be filled with the words 'is your favourite', so you write:

Example: | **0** | IS YOUR FAVOURITE

In the exam, you write only the missing words **IN CAPITAL LETTERS on a separate answer sheet.**

---

25 Denise always keeps her mobile switched on because David may need to contact her.

CASE

Denise never switches her mobile .... needs to contact her.

26 A man at the museum entrance gave us a map.

GIVEN

We .... a man at the museum entrance.

27 'Don't touch the plate, it's very hot,' the waitress said to me.

NOT

The waitress .... the plate because it was very hot.

28 Chris doesn't type as fast as his secretary.

TYPIST

Chris' secretary is .... than he is.

29 This cold weather probably won't last for more than a week.

UNLIKELY

This cold weather .... for more than a week.

30 It isn't easy for Zoe to answer the telephone in Spanish.

DIFFICULTY

Zoe .... the telephone in Spanish.

You are going to read an extract from a magazine article about a language course. For questions **31 – 36**, choose the answer (**A**, **B**, **C** or **D**) which you think fits best according to the text.

In the exam, you mark your answers **on a separate answer sheet**.

Travelling to Learn

Rather late in life, I decided it was time to master another language. Rather than dusting off my schoolgirl French, I opted for a clean break and took up Spanish. Three years of evening classes later, thanks to the enthusiastic teacher's efforts I could order a restaurant meal and ask for directions, but my conversational skills were limited to asking everybody how many brothers and sisters they had. The only true way to master a language is to live and breathe it for a period of time, and I toyed with the idea of taking a language 'immersion' course abroad, but two little words always stopped me: home stay. Then I saw that a tour operator had started offering such courses in Peru. The opportunity to realise two long-held ambitions in one holiday – to improve my Spanish and to see Machu Picchu – proved irresistible.

Any misgivings I have about the accommodation evaporate the moment I'm met by my home-stay family, the Rojas, at Cusco airport. They greet me warmly, like an old friend. Carlos is an optician and Carmucha owns a restaurant. With their four children, they live in a comfortable house right in the city centre. Then I'm whisked off to a family friend's birthday party, where I understand nothing apart from the bit where they sing Happy Birthday. By the end of the evening, my face aches from holding an expression of polite, but uncomprehending interest, and I fall into bed thinking, 'What have I let myself in for?'

The following morning, I'm off to school and get to know my new school friends. We're aged between 19 and 65, each spending up to a month studying before travelling around Peru. We had all clearly hit it off with our new families, though one of us is a bit alarmed at the blue flame that jumps out of the shower switch in the morning, one of us has a long bus ride in to the school, and another is disconcerted to find that his host mother is actually six years younger than him. We're all keen to meet our teachers and see which class we'll be joining. But after sitting the placement test, we learn that as it's not yet high season and the school isn't too busy, tuition will be one-on-one. Some find the prospect daunting, wondering if they'll be able to cope, but to my mind this is a pretty impressive student-teacher ratio, and I'm keen to make the most of it.

As the week unfolds, I slip into a routine. Four hours of classes in the morning, back home for lunch, then afternoons free for sightseeing. Cusco will supply anything it can to lure students away from their homework. It's all too easy to swap verb conjugations for a swift coffee in a bar, but it's three days before anybody comes up with the suggestion that maybe we don't have to go back to our respective families for dinner every night. Once the seed of rebellion has been planted, it takes hold. We take it in turns to pluck up the courage to ring our 'Mums' and ask if we can stay out late – rather strange when you consider that our average age is probably thirty-three. But after one rather unsatisfying restaurant meal, I decide that true authenticity is back home at the dinner table with Carmucha. As the week wears on, a strange thing starts to happen: the dinner-table chatter, which at first was so much 'white noise', starts to have some meaning and, miraculously, I can follow the thread of the conversation.

31   How did the writer feel after her evening classes?

    A   proud of what she'd learnt so far.

    B   frustrated at her slow rate of progress.

    C   critical of the attitude adopted by her teacher.

    D   unwilling to perform simple tasks in the language.

32   What put the writer off the idea of doing an 'immersion' course?

    A   having relatively little time to devote to it

    B   the thought of staying with a host family

    C   her own lack of fluency in the language

    D   the limited range of locations available

33   How did the writer feel after the party she attended?

    A   upset that people assumed she could speak Spanish.

    B   confident that she was beginning to make progress.

    C   unsure how well she would cope during her stay.

    D   worried that she may have seemed rude.

34   What did the writer discover when she met her fellow students?

    A   Some were less happy with the arrangements than she was.

    B   They would all be studying together for a fixed period.

    C   Some were much older than teachers at the school.

    D   They didn't all like their host families.

35   The word 'daunting' (line **20**) suggests that other students viewed one-to-one lessons as

    A   a disappointing change of plan.

    B   good value for money.

    C   an unexpected bonus.

    D   a difficult challenge.

36   How did the writer feel when her fellow students suggested a night out together?

    A   embarrassed by their immaturity

    B   keen not to offend her hosts

    C   amused by their behaviour

    D   unsure if she'd take part

Part 6

You are going to read an article about the use of robots. Six sentences have been removed from the article. Choose from the sentences **A – G** the one which fits each gap (**37 – 42**). There is one extra sentence you do not need to use.

In the exam, you mark your answers **on a separate answer sheet**.

If you're happy, the robot knows it

Robots are gaining the ability to engage us emotionally, giving them a much broader range of uses.

RoCo is what's called an expressive computer. It has a monitor for a head and a simple LCD screen for a face. Inhabiting a back room in the Massachusetts Institute of Technology's media lab, RoCo has a double-jointed neck, which allows it to shift the monitor up and down, tilt it forward and back and move it from side to side.

37 When you hang your head and sink into your chair, RoCo tilts forward and drops low to almost touch the desk, mimicking your gloomy posture. When you perk up and straighten your back, it spots the change and cheerfully swings forward and upward.

RoCo was unveiled at a human-robot interaction conference in Washington DC. Because it responds to a user's changes in posture, its creators hope people might be more likely to build up a relationship with the computer that will make sitting at a desk all day a little more enjoyable. **38**

The team is among a growing number of researchers who are investigating how far a robot's physical presence can influence people. **39** Researchers at Stanford University in California have already proved that an in-car assistance system, for example, can make us drive more carefully if the voice matches our mood. But robots can have a greater impact. 'If it can actually touch you, it's a lot more meaningful,' says Cynthia Breazeal of the Media Lab, who created RoCo with her colleague Rosalind Picard.

Breazeal suggests that RoCo could be programmed to adopt the right posture to foster greater attention and persistence in children. **40** To find out, Aaron Powers at iRobot in Burlington, Massachusetts, and colleagues at Carnegie Mellon University in Pittsburgh, Pennsylvania, invited volunteers to chat about health and happiness with a 1.3-metre-tall, talking humanoid robot called Pearl. They then compared their impressions with those of people who had only heard the robot and seen its projected image.

They found that volunteers rated the physical robot as more trustworthy, sociable, responsive, competent, respectful and lifelike than the projected image of the robot. More importantly, the researchers also found that the physical robot had the most influence over the volunteers. **41** This persuasive power is important and is already being put to use in the classroom. The emphasis is now on the improvement of teamwork and task coordination between humans and robots. But the idea of robots as teammates is not universally accepted. **42** Breazeal argues that this can be resolved by training people and robots together, so that we learn the robot's limitations in advance. 'There might be initial disappointment, but five minutes later we will have figured it out,' she says.

A But does a physical robot really provoke a greater response in people than a much cheaper animated agent on a computer screen could?

B An attached camera can detect when the user changes position, allowing RoCo to adjust its posture accordingly.

C This does not mean that the robots of the future may be able to see things from our point of view and correct us when we make bad decisions.

D Using technology to manipulate someone or shape their mood is nothing new.

E Because robots have no drive to protect themselves, they cannot protect the group, says Victoria Groom, a researcher in human-robot interaction.

F The robot had actually prompted lots of participants to declare that they would take up more healthy activities such as exercising and avoiding fatty foods.

G They also believe that by tuning into users' moods, the robot might help them to get their work done more effectively.

Part 7

You are going to read a magazine article about wild camping. For questions **43 – 52**, choose from the graduates (**A – D**). The campers may be chosen more than once.

In the exam, you mark your answers **on a separate answer sheet**.

Which camper …

enjoys the idea of facing some risks whilst camping?	**43**	
compares attitudes to wild camping now and in the past?	**44**	
is unwilling to recommend areas suitable for wild camping?	**45**	
is pleased to have shown others how to enjoy camping?	**46**	
refers to the need to travel light when camping?	**47**	
says a negative experience made camping seem unappealing for a while?	**48**	
says more people are beginning to see the attraction of wild camping ?	**49**	
describes a dangerous situation which could have been avoided?	**50**	
says inexperienced campers shouldn't go to remote places?	**51**	
gives reasons for disliking organised campsites?	**52**	

Wild camping

Camping in the wild rather than at organised campsites is a great way of getting away from it all. Four experienced wild campers tell us why.

A   Luis Gallivan

I'm turning my back on organised sites, particularly the super-sized ones. Even at the relatively quiet sites you can seldom escape the constant chattering of people in neighbouring tents, or worse still, the noise of satellite TVs in camper vans. I go wild camping, which means I can set up my tent in a field or on a mountainside without paying anyone for the privilege. Lots of 'mild campers' (that's what we call the ones who use campsites) are waking up to the fact that wild camping gives you an eco-friendly break and offers a great deal more in the way of adventure. Because it's so different from 'mild' camping, though, people need to ask themselves: 'Do I really need this?' before packing their stuff. Wild camping is the ultimate budget holiday – once you've got to wherever you're going, the only expense is feeding yourself.

B   Anna Cresswell

My first experience of wild camping was a bit of an accident. I'd trekked with a friend to a remote spot but we each had different plans. She wanted to stay the night in a tent, whilst I wanted to head back home before bedtime. As it happened, I was so exhausted that I ended up sharing the tiny uncomfortable tent with her. I must say the memory of that put me off wild camping for months, until I reminded myself that if I hadn't stayed, I'd never have witnessed that breath-taking sunset which more than made up for all the discomfort. Then there's the excitement that comes from making yourself slightly vulnerable: out in the wild with nobody watching over you. And I never have to book. If the weather's disappointing, I don't go. If it turns cold, I go home. This is as stress-free as holidays get.

C   Thomas Parsons

Perhaps the main reason many people shy away from wild camping is our modern-day culture of 'risk aversion' – in other words, avoiding all activities that seem in any way dangerous, however unlikely it is that anything would actually go wrong. In less paranoid times, wild camping was indeed very common, but people nowadays want safe environments, especially when it comes to feeling at ease about what their kids are doing, and organised campsites are the obvious answer. I'm not keen to suggest good places to go wild camping, though, because one of the joys of the activity comes from finding places nobody else knows about. For the beginner, I'd advise places which aren't too far from civilisation in case anything does go wrong.

D   Jennie Martinez

Camping was an integral part of my early years, and I've managed to pass on some of my enthusiasm to my own children. In striving for little luxuries like hot showers, 'mild' campers miss out on the delights of wild camping. There are very comfortable state-of-the-art tents available nowadays if you want a bit of comfort, and they don't cost that much. Once you're hooked on wild camping, nothing else will do and you get not to mind occasional problems with ants or wasps. The lack of fellow travellers makes me feel that the great views and the star-lit skies have been laid on expressly for my own personal enjoyment. But camping in wild places also means having to observe a few basic rules. For instance, during a particularly dry season, it's best to avoid high fire-risk areas. I'll always remember a time when I was camping with friends and we noticed that somebody had failed to extinguish a small fire completely. We managed to put it out, but it could have been a disaster.

Part 1

You **must** answer this question. Write your answer in **140 – 190** words in an appropriate style.

1 In your English class you have been discussing different ways of learning new things. Now your English teacher has asked you to write an essay.

Write an essay using **all** the notes and giving reasons for your point of view.

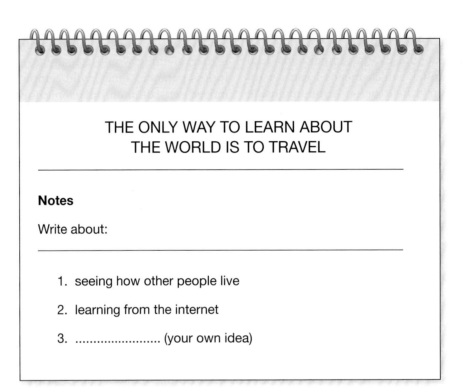

THE ONLY WAY TO LEARN ABOUT
THE WORLD IS TO TRAVEL

Notes

Write about:

1. seeing how other people live

2. learning from the internet

3. .... (your own idea)

Write your **essay**.

Write an answer to **one** of the questions **2 – 4** in this part. Write your answer in **140 – 190** words in an appropriate style.

2   You have seen an announcement in an English language magazine called *Leisure Time*.

> # *MY FAVOURITE SPORT*
>
> **Tell us about your favourite sport, when you started playing it, and if you would recommend it to people who want to make new friends.**
>
> ***The best article will get a surprise gift.***

Write your **article**.

3   This is part of an email you have received from a friend.

> When you wrote last, you said you had just started a summer job. How is it going? Is it hard working in the summer? Do you get any free time? Are the wages good?

Write your **email**

4   You recently attended a three-day cookery course at a local college.
Now the college magazine has asked you to write a report, addressing the following points.

1. the dishes they taught you to cook
2. how useful you found the course
3. whether you would recommend it to beginners of all ages

Write your **report**.

You will hear people talking in eight different situations. For questions **1 – 8**, choose the best answer (**A**, **B** or **C**).

1   You hear a woman talking about the final episode of a TV series.
     What does she say about it?
     A   It wasn't as good as previous episodes.
     B   It failed to attract large number of viewers.
     C   It delivered an unexpected end to the story.

2   You hear a dance club DJ talking about his work.
     What makes him unhappy?
     A   being asked to play old-fashioned types of music
     B   being asked to play the same track more than once
     C   being asked to play the bands which he dislikes most

3   You hear a man talking about an art exhibition.
     What does he criticise about it?
     A   the way the paintings were displayed
     B   the number of paintings in the exhibition
     C   the lack of information about the paintings

4   You hear a radio announcement about a job vacancy.
     What skill must you have if you want the job?
     A   an ability to deal with complaints
     B   an ability to work with numbers
     C   an ability to write well

5   You hear part of an interview with a restaurant owner.
     What is attracting customers to the restaurant?
     A   a website
     B   magazine reviews
     C   personal recommendations

6   You hear a young man talking about a recent trip.
     What was the main benefit of the trip for him?
     A   He became more independent.
     B   He learnt a foreign language.
     C   He made new friends.

7   You hear a sports journalist talking about an article she's written.
     What is the article about?
     A   the history of sport
     B   the benefits of sports
     C   the lack of sports facilities

8   You hear a young man talking about going camping.
     What is his advice?
     A   take a good variety of foodstuffs
     B   go prepared for bad weather
     C   choose the area carefully

Part 2

You will hear part of a programme about the history of roller skating. For questions **9 – 18**, complete the sentences with a word or short phrase.

History of roller skating

The country where the first roller skates were made was

(9) ....

In 1760, John Merlin went to a ball in London playing a

(10) .... whilst on roller skates.

Unfortunately, John Merlin injured himself when he broke a

(11) .... at a ball.

In Germany, roller skating was used in a ballet called

(12) ....

James Plimpton's invention helped roller skaters to control the

(13) .... of their skates.

The first team sport to be played on roller skates was

(14) ....

In Detroit in 1937, the first (15) ....

in the sport took place.

The use of plastics meant that both the (16) .... and ....

of roller skates improved.

The musical *Starlight Express* was seen by as many as

(17) .... in London.

The speaker says that modern roller skates are now

(18) .... and .... than ever before.

Part 3

You will hear five short extracts in which students are talking about their first year at university. For questions **19 – 23**, choose from the list (**A – H**) what each student says. There are three extra letters which you do not need to use.

A   I had to face some criticism when I chose a subject to study.

B   I was able to change an earlier decision about my studies.

Speaker 1 [ ] 19

C   I'm pleased that I'm able to combine studying with a job.

Speaker 2 [ ] 20

D   I had to be careful when choosing which college to study at.

Speaker 3 [ ] 21

E   It took time to get used to living in student accommodation.

Speaker 4 [ ] 22

F   I'm happy to have an active social life while at college.

Speaker 5 [ ] 23

G   I had to give up a good job to concentrate on my studies.

H   I was surprised to meet students from my old school here.

You will hear an interview with the film actor, Mikey Standish. For questions **24 – 30**, choose the best answer (**A**, **B** or **C**).

---

24   Mikey feels it is unfair when people suggest that

   A   some types of role are unsuitable for him.

   B   he's trying to imitate other well-known actors.

   C   he always plays rather similar characters.

25   How did Mikey feel while playing the character called Simon?

   A   sorry that he had decided to accept it

   B   confident that he knew Simon's character

   C   worried that Simon was so similar to himself

26   What kind of role does Mikey now refuse to play?

   A   weak people who become heroes

   B   the male lead in romantic films

   C   characters who do not change at all

27   Why did Mikey decide to go to drama school?

   A   It had been a long-held ambition.

   B   He felt he had no other option.

   C   A film director suggested it.

28   Mikey recommends that young people interested in acting go to drama school because

   A   it allows them to compare their skills with others.

   B   it teaches them to be competitive in the real world.

   C   it helps them decide whether acting is right for them.

29   What does Mikey say about his celebrity status?

   A   It was hard to get used to at first.

   B   It's making him increasingly uncomfortable.

   C   It has tended to come about gradually.

30   What are Mikey's immediate plans for the future?

   A   to take a break from film acting

   B   to write the script for a film

   C   to direct a film himself

Part 1 (2 minutes)

The examiner will ask you a few questions about yourself and what you think about different things. For example, the examiner might ask you about:

Education and work

- Do you like reading newspapers or magazines? (Why? / Why not?)
- Do you ever have to study / work hard at weekends? (Why? / Why not?)
- How often do you use a computer at work / college? (Tell us what you do.)
- Do you like working in a team at college / in your job? (Why / Why not?)

Holidays

- Where do you like to spend your holidays? (Why?)
- Do you like camping holidays? (Why? / Why not?)
- What country would you like to visit on holiday? (Why?)
- Do you prefer to travel with family or with friends? (Why?)

Celebrations

- Would you like to do something special for your next birthday? (Why? / Why not?)
- What special occasions did you enjoy most when you were a child? (Why?)
- Do you have street parties in your country? (Tell us about it.)
- Do you prefer big parties or small ones? (Why?)

Part 2 (4 minutes)

I'm going to give each of you two photographs. I'd like you to talk about your photographs on your own for about a minute, and also to answer a question about your partner's photographs.

(Candidate A), it's your turn first. Look at the photographs on page 175. They show **people and animals**. I'd like you to compare the photographs, and say **how the people and the animals may be feeling**. All right?

Thank you. *(Candidate B)*, **do you like animals?**

Now, *(Candidate B)*, look at your photogrpahs on page 176. They show **people playing different musical instruments**. I'd like you to compare the photographs, and say **how much the people may be enjoying the experience.**

Thank you. *(Candidate A)*, **can you play an instrument?**

Part 3 (4 minutes)

Now I'd like you to talk about something together for about two minutes.

I'd like you to imagine that you're going to give a talk to a class of eleven-year-olds about how to look after the environment. Here are some ideas you may want to include, and a question for you to discuss. First you have some time to look at the task on page 177.

Now talk to each other about **how appealing these ideas would be for the children.**

Now you have a minute to decide **which idea the children would find most difficult to understand.**

Part 4 (4 minutes)

Use the following questions in order, as appropriate:

- **How easy is it to recycle things in your area?**
- **Where should kids learn about the environment, at home or at school? (Why?)**
- **How easy do you think it would be talking to a class of eleven year-olds? (Why? / Why not?)**
- **At what age should children start to learn about the environment? (Why?)**
- **How difficult do you think it is for people to find reliable information about the environment?**
- **Some people say global warming is a serious problem. What's your opinion?**

> *Select any of the following prompts, as appropriate:*
>
> - **What do you think?**
> - **Do you agree?**
> - **And you?**

Thank you. That is the end of the test.

Part I

For questions **1 – 8**, read the text below and decide which answer (**A**, **B**, **C** or **D**) best fits each gap. There is an example at the beginning (**0**).

In the exam, you mark your answers **on a separate answer sheet**.

Example:

| 0 | **A** puts | **B** sets | **C** places | **D** fetches |

| 0 | **A** ▬ **B** ▭ **C** ▭ **D** ▭ |

Lunch is for sharing

Mimi Ito carefully **(0)** .... together her children's packed lunches each morning. She then takes photos of them and **(1)** .... these on her online blog. In this way, Mimi is able to **(2)** .... a record of meals that she's **(3)** .... of, and everyone has the chance to look at her mouth-watering creations. For these are no ordinary lunches, Mimi prepares what are **(4)** .... as bento meals for her children.

A bento is a single-portion Japanese takeaway meal that traditionally **(5)** .... of rice, fish or meat, with vegetables on the side. In Japan, they are normally served in distinctive trays divided into sections for the different parts of the meal. Mimi thinks that children in **(6)** .... enjoy having small compartments with little bits of food that are **(7)** .... to their small appetites. Mimi was born in Japan and currently lives in the USA. She is fairly health **(8)** .... , but believes that having wide tastes and finding pleasure in food is important.

1	**A** mails	**B** sends	**C** posts	**D** delivers
2	**A** make	**B** keep	**C** save	**D** do
3	**A** content	**B** satisfied	**C** proud	**D** pleased
4	**A** titled	**B** called	**C** named	**D** known
5	**A** consists	**B** includes	**C** contains	**D** involves
6	**A** specific	**B** particular	**C** special	**D** precise
7	**A** suited	**B** fitted	**C** created	**D** designed
8	**A** sensible	**B** conscious	**C** knowledgeable	**D** informed

For questions **9 – 16**, read the text below and think of the word which best fits each gap. Use only **one** word in each gap. There is an example at the beginning (**0**).

In the exam, you write your answers **IN CAPITAL LETTERS on a separate answer sheet**.

Example: | **0** | O | N | E | | | | | | | | | | | | | | | | | |

Mr Bean

The comedy character Mr Bean is **(0)** .... of Britain's most successful exports. Played by the actor Rowan Atkinson, Mr Bean is instantly recognisable to people around the world. The original television show has been shown on **(9)** .... than two-hundred TV stations, as **(10)** .... as on over fifty airlines.

So why is Mr Bean so popular? **(11)** .... many people regard Mr Bean as a typically British character, the initial inspiration actually came from a French comic character called Monsieur Hulot, created by the French comedian Jacques Tati.

According **(12)** .... Rowan Atkinson, however, the actual character of Mr Bean is mostly based on **(13)** .... own personality as a nine-year-old. Mr Bean is a man **(14)** .... is awkward, self-conscious and accident-prone. He's very selfish and doesn't really understand much about the world **(15)** .... him. He's really a child in a man's body. This is the basis for a lot of visual comedy and Atkinson mentions comedians **(16)** .... as Charlie Chaplin and Stan Laurel as other famous examples.

Part 3

For questions **17 – 24**, read the text below. Use the word given in capitals at the end of some of the lines to form a word that fits in the gap **in the same line**. There is an example at the beginning (**0**).

In the exam, you write your answers **IN CAPITAL LETTERS on a separate answer sheet**.

Example: | 0 | A | R | T | I | S | T | I | C | | | | | | | | | |

Computer Games

To get an idea of the (**0**) .... and technical skill that goes into a computer game, you only need to visit the Los Angeles studio of Electronic Arts, one of the world's largest and most (**17**) .... game-makers. The firm's (**18**) .... team have just started work on the latest version of one of their most popular games. As you enter the building, you see an (**19**) .... display of photographs that help you to imagine what the game's particular look and style will be like.

ARTIST

INFLUENCE

CREATE

IMPRESS

The (**20**) .... of the game will involve engineers, technical experts and musicians, and will cost millions of dollars. These days, there is a great deal of (**21**) .... between making a game and making a Hollywood movie, and it's big business.

DEVELOP

SIMILAR

According to (**22**) .... , Americans are spending increasing amounts of money on computer games each year. Part of the (**23**) .... for the success of the games comes from the (**24**) .... rise in the number of adults who are buying them, not as gifts for teenagers, but for their own personal use.

ECONOMY

EXPLAIN

EXPECTED

For questions **25 – 30**, complete the second sentence so that it has a similar meaning to the first sentence, using the word given. **Do not change the word given.** You must use between **two** and **five** words, including the word given. Here is an example (**0**).

Example:

0   What type of music do you like best?

FAVOURITE

What .... type of music?

The gap can be filled with the words 'is your favourite', so you write:

Example: | **0** | *IS YOUR FAVOURITE*

In the exam, you write **only** the missing words **IN CAPITAL LETTERS on a separate answer sheet.**

---

25   Which of the places you visited interested you most?

THE

Which was .... that you visited?

26   Sally arrived late at the conference because her flight was delayed.

TIME

If Sally's .... , she wouldn't have arrived late at the conference.

27   Colin will only read your email immediately if you mark it as urgent.

UNLESS

Colin will .... you mark it as urgent.

28   Tania regrets lending her new laptop to her little brother.

WISHES

Tania .... her new laptop to her little brother.

29   I'm sure it was a real disappointment for Gerry that his team didn't win promotion.

BEEN

Gerry .... that his team didn't win promotion.

30   Alex offered Cindy a lift on his new motorbike, but she didn't accept.

TURNED

Cindy .... offer of a lift on his new motorbike.

You are going to read an extract from a novel. For questions **31 – 36**, choose the answer (**A**, **B**, **C** or **D**) which you think fits best according to the text.

In the exam, you mark your answers **on a separate answer sheet**.

I made a discovery on the way to Ruth's aunt's house in Spain. The things you worry about don't always turn out as badly as you expect. Sometimes they're worse. Everything would have been different if our plane had landed on schedule. Ruth was quite nice about it, as always, but I know that she really thought it was my fault.

Our plan had been to arrive in Spain, collect the hire car, shop for groceries and still get to the house in daylight. I'd felt proud of myself when I'd booked the tickets. I'd got a special cheap offer on the internet. But that was silly because Ruth's aunt was paying our expenses and she wasn't the kind of woman who expects people to fly on budget airlines. To her mind, you pay full price for comfort and reliability. Our flight got to Spain about three hours later than expected.

By the time we got to where our hire-car was waiting amongst dozens of others, it was totally dark. The man at the desk confirmed what we'd guessed. It was too late for shopping. While I signed for the car – gripping the pen hard so that my name wouldn't look as shaky as I felt – Ruth bought two cartons of fruit juice from a vending machine.

'Ruth!' I said, as I drove cautiously out of the car park, gripping the wheel. 'Which way is it? I'm not going to be able to understand any of the road signs!'

13 'You just need to follow the coast road,' said Ruth. 'It's simple. Things don't get tough until we take a left into the mountains.'

As all I had to do was drive straight ahead, I began to relax. Then it was time to turn off into the mountains and I felt stressed again. Apart from anything else, you don't get street lighting on lonely country roads in southern Spain. This road climbed slowly but steadily in a series of Z-shapes, with a rocky wall on the left and a steep drop on the right. We gradually lost the rest of the traffic until there was hardly any. I can tell you now that hardly any is worse than a lot. All would be quiet and then suddenly headlights would appear behind us, sweep past us and vanish. Or lights would blaze round a corner ahead, without warning, looking as though they were coming right at us.

Ruth read out where I should go, and me and the car went. It all made sense. Or it did until she pointed to an olive grove, all silvery in the moonlight, and told me to drive into it.

'I can't,' I said. 'There's no road.'

'There's a track,' said Ruth. 'Up ahead, see? On the left. It's right opposite a white house with green shutters, just like the directions say.'

I gave way. But I wasn't happy. 'This is not a track,' I said, driving cautiously onto it. 'It's just a strip of land where the olive trees aren't.' We bounced slowly along in silence, apart from the scrunching of pebbles under the wheels. Ahead was the dark outline of a small house.

'This is it,' said Ruth. 'See – we made it!'

The track opened out into a parking space beside the house. There it stopped – end of the road. 'Are you sure about this?' I whispered. 'It's really late, Ruth. If we're wrong, we're going to wake people up.'

'There's no one to wake up,' said Ruth, getting out. 'The place is empty. Just waiting for us.'

31   What does the narrator suggest about her trip in the first paragraph?

    A   She'd expected Ruth to share the blame for what happened.

    B   She'd expected Ruth to be angry with her.

    C   She'd expected aspects of it to go wrong.

    D   She'd expected her plane to be delayed.

32   What mistake did the narrator make when booking their flight?

    A   She hadn't followed Ruth's advice about the airline.

    B   She'd forgotten that someone else was paying for them.

    C   She'd chosen one that was scheduled to arrive after dark.

    D   She hadn't realised that they would need to go shopping on arrival.

33   How did the narrator feel in the car-hire office?

    A   keen not to let her nervous state show

    B   cross because she had to wait in a queue

    C   grateful for the advice of the man behind the desk

    D   confused by the documents that she needed to sign

34   'it' in line **13** refers to

    A   understanding the road signs.

    B   driving in the dark.

    C   taking a left turn.

    D   finding the way.

35   When driving into the mountains, the narrator felt

    A   reassured by the sound of passing traffic.

    B   alarmed by the sight of other car headlights.

    C   frustrated by their rather slow progress.

    D   unsure if they were on the right road.

36   How did Ruth know that they should turn into the olive grove?

    A   She was consulting a map.

    B   She had been there before.

    C   She had written instructions.

    D   She asked some local residents.

Part 6

You are going to read an article about a musician. Six sentences have been removed from the article. Choose from the sentences **A – G** the one which fits each gap (**37 – 42**). There is one extra sentence you do not need to use.

In the exam, you mark your answers **on a separate answer sheet**.

Femi Kuti, a great African musician

In the fashion-led world of pop culture, carrying a famous name is always a burden, as the offspring of musicians like John Lennon and Bob Marley have found. Yet the history of much of the world's music – certainly in Africa – is based on a long and deep tradition of passing on the torch from one generation to the next. Femi Kuti is the son of Fela Kuti, a renowned musician who died ten years ago.

Throughout his career, Femi Kuti has had to suffer comparisons with his father. You can't fill the boots of a legend and Fela Kuti was not only an extraordinary and innovative musician but one of the giants of world music. **37** He has kept alive the flame of Afro-beat as well as bringing his own unique creativity to its rhythms.

Femi was born in London in 1962, when his father was a student at the Royal Academy. Fela never showed his oldest son any signs of approval or encouragement. **38** Yet by the age of fifteen, Femi's impressive playing had earned him a place in his father's band, Egypt 80, on merit.

Femi didn't have to wait long for his first opportunity to head that band. In 1985, it had been booked to play at the Hollywood Bowl, but Femi's father failed to make it on to the plane. **39** This gave him the confidence he needed to start a band of his own.

In 1986, together with keyboard player Dele Sosimi, Femi left his father's band and formed the band *Positive Force*, resulting in tensions between father and son that were to last several years. **40** Now a collector's item, its mix of funk, soul and jazz, driven by thundering percussion, proved that he could stand on his own two feet.

Femi made his first US tour in 1995, which culminated in an acclaimed appearance at the Summer stage in New York's Central Park in July. The tour coincided with the release of his album, Femi Kuti, which earned him very good reviews across Europe and the US. **41** He finally admitted that his son had what it takes.

Though Femi remains resentful of what he sees as his father's lack of support early in his career, he recognises that he learnt things from him: ' **42** ' says Femi. That individuality was certainly evident on his next album, *Shoki Shoki*, which added fresh flavours drawn from contemporary R&B and dance music.

And as we wait for his next album, the Kuti tradition continues and Femi's own son now plays alongside him in *Positive Force*. 'The one thing I learned from my father was to be true to myself, and that's the advice I've given my own child.' Femi sounds proud of his son.

A   Femi stepped forward to fill his place, and did so, by all accounts, with considerable skill.

B   It also won him six awards at Nigeria's Fame Music Awards and led at last to a reconciliation with his father.

C   Yet his father's long shadow should not obscure the fact that Femi Kuti has developed into a fine performer in his own right.

D   It was at this place that he helped to fund a variety of cultural, social and educational projects.

E   Femi's debut album with the new band, No Cause for Alarm?, was recorded in Lagos and released on Polygram Nigeria in 1987.

F   After giving him a saxophone as a young boy, he then refused to give him any lessons.

G   When I look at his life, it's very hard for me to be angry with him because he taught me to be different and to do things my own way.

Part 7

You are going to read an article about extreme sports. For questions **43 – 52**, choose from the graduates (**A – D**). The graduates may be chosen more than once.

In the exam, you mark your answers **on a separate answer sheet**.

Which person ...

was aware of making a mistake during training?	**43**
expected the first day of training to be relatively easy?	**44**
was confident of having the physical strength to succeed?	**45**
Improved their performance by following some useful advice?	**46**
Is confident of overcoming any feelings of fear?	**47**
felt nervous when preparing to try the sport for the first time?	**48**
mentions the feeling of joy that the sport gave?	**49**
was told the sport was not as dangerous as people think?	**50**
was more successful than somebody else in a first attempt?	**51**
felt disappointed when the trainer gave an order to stop?	**52**

ANYONE FOR EXTREME SPORTS?

Tired of going to the gym? Why not try something you might actually enjoy? Four courageous people describe their own choices …

A   Brenda Gordon: flying trapeze

I wanted to do something where I was having so much fun I wouldn't even notice I was exercising. I decided to try a half-day circus-skills course. Despite doing a series of preparation exercises, when I stood facing the flying trapeze, I noticed a slight fluttering in my stomach. Next, I was shown the right way to grip the trapeze and how to step off the platform without hitting my back. Then, suddenly, I was being counted down from three. My heart was racing but I kept thinking I'd no doubt be able to take my body weight in my very muscular arms. Then in a moment, I'd stepped off and, incredibly, I was swinging through the air. It was exhilarating, and I was aware of a real feeling of regret when the instructor told me to drop. A year later, I'm a fearless trapeze flyer, though my muscles still hurt after every session.

B   Guy Stanton: ice-climbing

I started ice-climbing at an indoor climbing centre with an enormous artificial ice cave. I turned up fully kitted up in climbing boots, metal crampons and two metal ice axes. The instructor ran through a demonstration. Then it was my turn. I buried the axes in the ice, kicked one boot at the wall, then the other, and started climbing. But I had forgotten my first important lesson: don't bury your axes too deep. As my desire not to fall increased, so I hammered them deeper until they got stuck. My arms were aching and I stopped, utterly disappointed with myself. The trainer shouted some encouragement: 'You can do it, don't grip the axes so hard!' I did so and my more relaxed style meant less pressure on my arms, so I started enjoying it. I still feel frightened when I'm high up, but I know I'll feel completely at ease eventually.

C   Debbie Bridge: free-diving

Free-diving consists of diving to great depths without an oxygen tank. I took part in a course organised by a leading sub-aqua website, which took place in a thirty-metre high, six-metre wide cylindrical water tank. Unlike me, who had never been deeper than the swimming-pool floor, my co-trainees were all scuba divers. Our trainer was keen to prove free-diving isn't so risky. 'When practised correctly, it's a very safe sport,' she said. After a few lectures about safety, and suitably kitted out in flippers and a diving mask, I was ready to get into the water. With a partner, we were going to attempt to descend and ascend by pulling on a rope. My partner dived first but had trouble and stopped at five metres. Then I dived, pulling myself downwards on the rope and reached fifteen metres easily, feeling more and more at ease. This sport isn't about adrenaline, it's about being calm.

D   Max Wainright: snowboarding

I'd always wanted to try snowboarding, so I went for a training day at an indoor snow slope near my home. Having had the pleasure of learning the basics of snowboarding several years before in the French Alps, I'd hoped that returning to the sport might be a bit like riding a bike, something you supposedly never forget. But it seemed that most of what I'd learned had melted away just like snow. I knew I shouldn't use the techniques I'd learnt in years of surfing and skiing because they weren't applicable to snowboarding at all. I started riding slowly at first, and couldn't get the balance right. It took hours before I could pick up speed and successfully perform a neat turn. But I was getting the hang of it! What a thrill to feel the cool air rushing by, what fun to crash into the snow!

Part 1

You **must** answer this question. Write your answer in **140 – 190** words in an appropriate style.

1   In your English class you have been discussing options for future work. Now your English teacher has asked you to write an essay.

Write an essay using **all** the notes and giving reasons for your point of view.

PEOPLE SHOULD DO A JOB THEY LOVE
AND NOT WORRY ABOUT MONEY

Notes

Write about:

1. being happy at work

2. the need to earn a living

3. .... (your own idea)

Write your **essay**.

Write an answer to **one** of the questions **2 – 4** in this part. Write your answer in **140 – 190** words in an appropriate style.

2   You have seen this advertisement and you want to apply.

> **Are you good at writing songs, singing or playing an instrument?**
>
> **At Heath College of Music we're looking for new talent!**
>
> We need enthusiastic people who are willing to devote many hours a day to studying. Write to Clara Barnes, the director, explaining
>
> • why you would want to attend a course,
> • what musical skills you have,
> • what your favourite music is.

Write your **letter**.

3   You recently saw this notice in the college magazine.

> # Do you watch an animated cartoon which is enjoyed by adults as well as children?
>
> Write us a review of the cartoon for the college magazine. Describe some of the characters, say what makes it funny and why you think older people like it too.
>
> **The best review will be published next month!**

Write your **review**.

4   You have read this announcement in an international magazine for English language students.

> # *Enter our Writing Competition!*
>
> Write an interesting article on this topic and you could win £200!
>
> **My childhood ambitions**
>
> • As a child, what job did you want to do in the future?
> • How did your ambitions change as you grew older?

Write your **article**.

Part 1

You will hear people talking in eight different situations. For questions **1 – 8**, choose the best answer (**A**, **B** or **C**).

1   You hear part of a programme about music in schools.
    Why are fewer children joining school choirs?
    A   They are unwilling to sing in public.
    B   Their parents don't encourage them to sing.
    C   Their teachers lack the necessary musical skills.

2   You hear two friends talking about evening classes.
    Why did the girl decide to register for a photography course?
    A   She wanted to take better holiday snaps.
    B   She thought it would help her in her career.
    C   She needed a relaxing change from her studies.

3   You hear two friends talking about a new café.
    What did they both approve of?
    A   the size of the portions
    B   the originality of the food
    C   the efficiency of the service

4   You hear part of a programme about exploring underground caves.
    What does the speaker do?
    A   He's an experienced caver.
    B   He's a journalist.
    C   He's a student.

5   You hear a woman talking about a job interview.
    What does she say about it?
    A   Some of the questions were unfair.
    B   She felt she was insufficiently prepared.
    C   The interviewers put her under pressure.

6   You hear a woman talking about a language course.
    What does she criticise about it?
    A   There are too many students.
    B   Grammar isn't focused on.
    C   It isn't challenging enough.

7   You hear part of a podcast on the subject of food.
    The speaker works as
    A   a shop owner.
    B   a cookery writer.
    C   a chef in a restaurant.

8   You hear a man talking about moving house.
    After moving to a new area, he felt
    A   worried that he wouldn't see his old friends.
    B   concerned about how his children would adapt.
    C   surprised by how welcoming his new neighbours were.

You will hear a woman called Rita Lewis giving a presentation about her job as a researcher for a TV programme. For questions **9 – 18**, complete the sentences with a word or short phrase.

Rita Lewis: TV researcher

The subject that Rita studied first at university was

(9) ....

Before getting her current job, Rita studied a subject called

(10) ....

On the day she tells us about, the country where Rita was working was

(11) ....

There were a total of **(12)** ....

people in Rita's team on that day.

The animal which the presenter called Jamie had to photograph was a sort of

(13) ....

The camera crew had to film Jamie as he climbed over the edge of a

(14) ....

Rita's lunch consisted of sandwiches with

(15) .... in them.

Jamie had to hold a **(16)** ....

to help him see the crocodiles as he crossed a river.

A special light which the crew was using, known as a

(17) .... , stopped working.

Rita says that Jamie looks really **(18)** ....

when you see him crossing the river on the programme.

You will hear five short extracts in which craft workers are talking about running their own small businesses from home. For questions **19 – 23**, choose from the list (**A – H**) the advice each speaker gives about running such a business. There are three extra letters which you do not need to use.

___

A   expand your business by advertising locally

B   don't be discouraged by negative customer feedback

Speaker 1		19

C   employ family and friends to market your product

Speaker 2		20

D   spend time organising your workspace properly

Speaker 3		21

E   increase business by selling online

Speaker 4		22

F   produce a clear marketing plan for your business

Speaker 5		23

G   continue to learn in order to perfect your product

H   pay for expert help if you get into difficulties

You will hear an interview with a woman called Monica Darcey, who's the author of a best-selling book about gardening. For questions **24 – 30**, choose the best answer (**A**, **B** or **C**).

24 Monica says that most people who buy her book

    A   have made mistakes in gardening.

    B   are knowledgeable about gardening.

    C   do not trust professional gardeners.

25 How did Monica's parents feel about her early interest in gardening?

    A   They were concerned about the effects on her health.

    B   They were worried that she lacked other interests.

    C   They feared her enthusiasm would affect her studies.

26 Monica applied to work as a gardening journalist because

    A   it would give her an extra source of income.

    B   she'd found the experience of writing rewarding.

    C   there might be opportunities to do some research.

27 Why did Monica give up her job on a magazine?

    A   She got an offer of work somewhere else.

    B   She didn't get on with other members of staff.

    C   She was not interested in the type of work she was doing.

28 According to Monica, what makes her gardening books special?

    A   They are written in an entertaining style.

    B   They are aimed at amateur enthusiasts.

    C   They are the result of detailed research.

29 What does Monica dislike about the photographs in many gardening books?

    A   They reduce the importance of the writer.

    B   They help to sell with poor quality writing.

    C   They show an unrealistic view of their subject.

30 What makes Monica unsure whether to accept a job on television?

    A   Her publisher may disapprove of it.

    B   It may make her suddenly famous.

    C   She would have less time for writing.

Part 1 (2 minutes)

The examiner will ask you a few questions about yourself and what you think about different things. For example, the examiner might ask you about:

Home and daily routine

- Do you listen to music in the evening? (Why? / Why not?)
- Do you usually have a small or a large breakfast? (What do you have?)
- How often do you see your friends outside college / work? (What do you do?)
- Are you happy with the size of your bedroom? (Why? / Why not?)

Media

- Do you watch a lot of television? (Why? / Why not?)
- How do you find out what's happening in the world?
- What type of magazines do you like reading? (Why?)
- How often do you use social media? (What do you use it for?)

Sport

- Would you rather do a team sport, or one you could do on your own? (Why?)
- Is there a place near your house where you can get some exercise? (Tell us about it.)
- Do you like to watch sports competitions? (Why? / Why not?)
- Is there a sports personality that you particularly admire? (Tell us about him/her.)

Part 2 (4 minutes)

I'm going to give each of you two photographs. I'd like you to talk about your photographs on your own for about a minute, and also to answer a question about your partner's photographs.

(Candidate A), look at page 178 and photographs which show **people using different types of transport**. I'd like you to compare the photographs, and say **why the people may have chosen to travel in this way**.

Thank you. *(Candidate B)*, **do you like travelling by bus?**

Now, *(Candidate B)*, turn to the photographs on page 179. They show **people playing different games**. I'd like you to compare the photographs, and say **how interesting these games would be for different age groups**.

Thank you. *(Candidate A)*, **do you like computer games?**

Part 3 (4 minutes)

Now I'd like you to talk about something together for about two minutes. Now look at page 180.

I'd like you to imagine that a group of students from another country is coming here on a visit. Here are some situations where they may need some advice, and a question for you to discuss. First you have some time to look at the task.

Now talk to each other about what advice you would give in these situations.

Thank you. Now you have a minute to decide **which is the most important to give advice about.**

Part 4 (4 minutes)

Use the following questions in order, as appropriate:

- **Do you think schools / colleges should organise group trips to other countries? (Why? / Why not?)**
- **Is it better to travel in a large group or a small group? (Why?)**
- **Is it important to speak the language of a country you visit? (Why? / Why not?)**
- **Some people say that travel is unnecessary because you can find out about other countries on the internet. What do you think?**
- **If you could spend a year in another country, which would you chose? Why?**
- **Some people say it's essential to plan a trip well in advance. What do you think?**

Thank you. That is the end of the test.

> *Select any of the following prompts, as appropriate:*
>
> - **What do you think?**
> - **Do you agree?**
> - **And you?**

TEST 5

Part 1

For questions **1 – 8**, read the text below and decide which answer (**A, B, C** or **D**) best fits each gap. There is an example at the beginning (**0**).

In the exam, you mark your answers **on a separate answer sheet**.

Example:

0   **A**   likes   **B**   insists   **C**   pretends   **D**   stresses

0	A	B	C	D

The world's finest chocolates

Belgium **(0)** .... to think of itself as the home of the finest chocolate in the world. If this **(1)** .... is true, then the Place du Grand Sablon in Brussels must be the centre of the chocolate world. This square isn't far from the city's museum of fine arts and some of the country's **(2)** .... chocolate shops can be found there.

Marcolini is a relatively recent arrival in the square and yet is **(3)** .... thought to be one of the most fashionable chocolate-makers in Belgium. The designers of the company's shop have evidently been **(4)** .... up ideas from Emporio Armani a few doors down. The Marcolini shop has black walls, a white floor and staff who **(5)** .... in black-and-white shirts and resemble fashion models **(6)** .... than salespeople.

When it comes to the chocolates themselves, these are displayed in impressive glass cases. Once you've **(7)** .... your selection, you go over to the counter to pay, and get a wonderful close-up **(8)** .... of a flowing fountain of melted chocolate.

1	**A** accusation	**B** claim	**C** demand	**D** challenge
2	**A** leading	**B** winning	**C** ruling	**D** beating
3	A wholly	B greatly	C widely	D deeply
4	A catching	**B** picking	**C** getting	**D** copying
5	**A** carry	B wear	C dress	D clothe
6	A instead	**B** otherwise	**C** whereas	**D** rather
7	A done	B achieved	C made	D arrived
8	A view	**B** scene	**C** sight	**D** glance

For questions **9 – 16**, read the text below and think of the word which best fits each gap. Use only **one** word in each gap. There is an example at the beginning (**0**).

In the exam, you write your answers **IN CAPITAL LETTERS on a separate answer sheet**.

Example: | **0** | W | I | T | H | | | | | | | | | | | | | | | |

Health on holiday

Nobody wants to deal **(0)** .... a medical emergency on holiday. In practice, however, you may not have **(9)** .... choice in the matter, and it's best to be prepared. If you're travelling independently that means taking a first aid kit.

The whole idea of the kit **(10)** .... that you can carry it around with you, so it needs to be both light and compact. You can buy a pre-prepared kit **(11)** .... includes the main essential items, and this should be adequate in most situations. The problems that you're most likely to encounter are minor cuts, stings and so **(12)** .... , and these can be sorted **(13)** .... easily enough.

Equally important is reading, and preferably packing, a good basic first aid book. This will help you to know **(14)** .... to do in any less familiar situations, and **(15)** .... best to deal with unexpected emergencies. Finally, keep your first-aid kit in a pocket or towards the top of your bag, just in **(16)** .... you need to find it in a hurry.

For questions **17 – 24**, read the text below. Use the word given in capitals at the end of some of the lines to form a word that fits in the gap **in the same line**. There is an example at the beginning (**0**).

In the exam, you write your answers **IN CAPITAL LETTERS on a separate answer sheet**.

Example:

| 0 | O | C | C | A | S | I | O | N | A | L | L | Y | | | | | |

Music and maths

As a teenager, I used to play the flute in my high-school orchestra. In much of the music that we played, the sound of the flute was needed only (**0**) .... So I spent a lot of my time during (**17**) .... counting the beats which the conductor indicated with each (**18**) .... of his baton.

OCCASION

PERFORM

MOVE

Those minutes spent reciting 'one, two, three, four' under my breath while the rest of the orchestra played seemed (**19**) .... to me. But they planted in my young brain the idea that there must be a (**20**) .... between music and numbers and I decided to do a bit of research in the school library.

END

CONNECT

I soon learnt that history is full of (**21**) .... to this idea, which had been a source of (**22**).......... for thinkers ever since the time of Pythagoras. Indeed an early book on music by the Ancient Roman philosopher Boethius is largely filled with diagrams and explanations about the (**23**) .... between music and mathematics. Out of the boredom of orchestra practice, an (**24**) .... new interest had emerged for me.

REFER

FASCINATE

RELATION

EXPECT

For questions **25 – 30**, complete the second sentence so that it has a similar meaning to the first sentence, using the word given. **Do not change the word given**. You must use between two and five words, including the word given. Here is an example (**0**).

Example:

0   What type of music do you like best?

FAVOURITE

What .... type of music?

The gap can be filled with the words 'is your favourite', so you write:

Example:	0	*IS YOUR FAVOURITE*

In the exam, you write **only** the missing words **IN CAPITAL LETTERS on a separate answer sheet.**

---

25   I had never been to that restaurant before.

FIRST

It .... I had ever been to that restaurant.

26   Luca was the only club member who hadn't paid his membership fees.

ALL

Apart .... the club members had paid their membership fees.

27   Simon doesn't object to his photograph appearing in the school brochure.

NO

Simon .... his photograph appearing in the magazine.

28   It is said that eating certain types of fish is very good for your health.

SUPPOSED

Eating certain types of fish .... very good for your health.

29   During the carnival, they didn't let people park in the city centre.

ALLOWED

In the city centre, parking .... the carnival was taking place.

30   Damian didn't buy a ticket because the machine wasn't working properly.

IF

Damian would have bought a ticket .... working properly.

You are going to read an extract from an article about a college. For questions **31 – 36**, choose the answer (**A**, **B**, **C** or **D**) which you think fits best according to the text.

In the exam, you mark your answers **on a separate answer sheet**.

The Cranston Institute of Modern Music

The Cranston Institute of Modern Music was set up after Toby Slocombe, guitarist with the rock band *Stanza*, often in the charts in the 1990s, decided to give up his job at a university music department, and set up something closer to his own heart. 'We have a more specialist niche here: we're more band, more rock'n'roll oriented. I was at a really good university, but we don't do technical stuff here – we want the substance, we look after the band-oriented people. We own it, and we set the culture, and that's great,' says Toby. Courses range from one-year diplomas to accredited degree courses, with students specialising in guitar, bass, drums or vocals, or focusing on the touring and management end of things. While the strings and percussion departments are male-dominated, two-thirds of the singers are female.

'The biggest myth musicians have is that someone will wave a magic wand and sort out the business side. Bands who make it actually accept responsibility for all aspects of what goes on,' says Toby. So, no matter what the student's speciality, their courses will include business modules. The story of popular music is full of stories about artists being
11 ripped off by shiny-suited managers. They are the people who produce contracts that you need a microscope to read and who retire to the Bahamas while their victims remain as poor as ever.

'There's a live performance workshop every week, for which students are given a song to learn,' says Tim Wethers, head of the guitar department. 'You'd expect something heavy to be the most popular track, but last year it was a really delicate song that people seemed to like the most. They were dreading it, but they were so pleased to get it right.'

Those weekly performances involve individuals from various disciplines being matched together, and that's how *The Omega Faction* became a unit last year, with singer Adam Omega hooking up with guitar, bass and drum contemporaries. 'I was into drum and bass and garage. Through some friends I heard about Cranston. As a singer, it's been fantastic: you learn technical exercises, warming up, keeping the voice healthy, the history of music, but the main thing for me is the live performance events. Learn a song, and then you're at a proper venue with a band. It's a place where you're all in the same boat, and it's competitive, but in a friendly way.'

The competition element peaks in the quest to appear on the annual compilation album: last year, 160 demos were sent in by students hoping to make the final cut of twelve. Cranston's principal is particularly pleased when diploma students' tracks show up on the playlist. 'Most of the students are full-time and from local schools,' he says. They're
25 often people who didn't really engage with school. You know they might end up quite disengaged from life otherwise, and it's great when they get on to the album and sound better than some of those from higher levels.'

Tutors, too, are on a learning curve. Members of staff undertake a two-year, part-time, special teaching course at Toby's old university. 'It's a bit like a football team here, with people fulfilling different roles,' he says. You've got your tutors who can transcribe the entire back catalogue of Frank Zappa, and then you've got your less academic but very
30 vociferous types. There's a constant turnover, with many going on the road, on tour to all sorts of places. Students like that – it shows them the facts of life as a musician.

31   Toby Slocombe likes his job better than his previous one because he's now able to

    A   attract students from other colleges.

    B   concentrate on one type of music.

    C   vary the content of the courses.

    D   reflect changes in technology.

32   The expression 'ripped off' in line **11** suggests that some artists are

    A   cheated in some way.

    B   given generous contracts.

    C   not as innocent as people think.

    D   able to make their own business deals.

33   Adam Omega says that what he appreciates most about Cranston is

    A   the mixture of styles it embraces.

    B   the prestige of the degrees it awards.

    C   the way it looks after artists' well-being.

    D   the opportunity to perform professionally.

34   The college principal uses the expression 'end up quite disengaged from life' (line **25**) to indicate that some students

    A   fail to appear on the compilation album.

    B   make more of an effort than others.

    C   need special support to succeed.

    D   come from broken homes.

35   Toby compares Cranston to a football club to suggest that members of staff want to

    A   encourage healthy competition.

    B   like travelling to represent the college.

    C   each have particular skills to offer.

    D   are very loyal to their institution.

36   The word 'many' in line **30** refers to

    A   facts.

    B   tutors.

    C   places.

    D   students.

Part 6

You are going to read an article about cryptozoology. Six sentences have been removed from the article. Choose from the sentences **A – G** the one which fits each gap (**37 – 42**). There is one extra sentence you do not need to use.

In the exam, you mark your answers **on a separate answer sheet**.

What is cryptozoology?

Is there such an animal as a yeti? Does Bigfoot really exist? Cryptozoology is the study of animal species that people claim to have seen, but which are as yet unknown to science. Some people call it a pseudoscience, but I object to that terminology because I'm not interested in ghost stories or UFOs. They're like a wisp of smoke compared to biological cases where I can find real evidence to back up what people say, such as hair, footprints or photographs. The goal of cryptozoology is to discover new species. The giant panda, the megamouth shark, and the Komodo dragon were all cryptozoological until the 20th century. **37** Now, they're accepted as zoological species.

Growing up, I never thought of myself as a zoologist or a biologist. **38** When I was twelve, I watched *Half Human*, a movie about the yeti. I asked my teachers about it, but they told me to get back to my schoolwork. So I went to the local library, where I found a limited number of books, but in them were the contact details of cryptozoologists to correspond with.

By the time I was fourteen, I was well known in the field; now I'm considered its elder statesman. I started writing articles, then books. But I wasn't just sitting in my room: I was with game wardens, investigating reports of phenomena such as mystery cats or giant snakes. I still do that today. For example, last summer residents of Westbrook, Maine, found a giant snakeskin. **39** Although I didn't find one, I commented on the case to the media and wrote articles about the long history of mysterious giant snakes, from the Giant Pennsylvania Snake sightings of the mid-1800s to the Peninsula Python sightings in Ohio in 1944.

Some of the sightings of these creatures are misidentifications. Bigfoot could be the back end of a moose or it could be a known animal in an unusual place. There have been fakes too. **40** If you listened to the media, however, you'd think it was a much higher figure.

I've written more than forty books about these animals, and I founded a museum devoted to them in Portland, Maine in the USA. We display artefacts such as a dart gun used to hunt Bigfoot from 1969 to 1973, footprint casts from Bigfoot and the yeti, and ephemera from famous movies. We also catalogue fakes. We have a Feejee mermaid: a half-monkey, half-fish that was fabricated in the 19th century and later exhibited in sideshows. We have a mask from the Georgia Bigfoot hoax of 2008, when an ape costume was passed off as a Bigfoot corpse. We also had a Bigfoot statue at one point. **41** Our mission is educational and scientific: we have a good relationship with the schools in Portland.

In the course of my career, I've run into two groups that I disagree with. The first were the debunkers who say that there's nothing out there. **42** These I call the 'true believers'. Every sound they hear in the woods is a Bigfoot. I surround myself with and identify with the people in the middle: the open-minded sceptics.

A   But members of the other one were just as closed-minded.

B   I believed that neither of these was real.

C   I've found, however, that these generally only account for around one per cent of all cases.

D   I went to the area to look for signs of the animal itself.

E   People had seen them, but their reports were dismissed as fantastical.

F   All our visitors were invited to take a picture of themselves with it.

G   What interested me more was the romantic aspects of natural history.

Part 7

You are going to read an article about careers in tourism. For questions **43 – 52**, choose from the people (**A – E**). The peole may be chosen more than once.

In the exam, you mark your answers **on a separate answer sheet**.

Which person ...

refers to a lack of outstanding professionals in one area of work?	**43**	
stresses the need to provide clients with a balance between freedom and control?	**44**	
regrets a decision made years ago?	**45**	
mentions the need to take the right decisions under pressure?	**46**	
says people shouldn't feel discouraged if they don't earn much initially?	**47**	
says larger companies are able to offer better conditions to workers?	**48**	
believes that qualifications alone won't get you promotion?	**49**	
recalls making a mistake whilst doing the job?	**50**	
says there are likely to be more chances to get training in future?	**51**	
warns about the decreasing job opportunities in one sector?	**52**	

What sort of person do you need to be to work in tourism?

A Claire Davies:
Receptionist in a five-star hotel

Claire says that what appeals to her most is the diversity of the challenges she faces every day – from dealing with phone calls in different languages to making bookings for restaurants. She first came to the hotel when she was on a year's work experience from university and now works part-time, which allows her to continue with her degree course in management. Her advice to anyone considering a career in hotels is not to be put off by the thought of low wages at the start. Having the right degree or diploma is no guarantee that you'll make your way up the career ladder, but the right attitude and good communication skills will get you a long way.

B Peter Gattoni:
Chef in an Italian restaurant

The place where Peter works attracts what's called the 'gourmet tourist', whose holiday is never complete without the opportunity to try out the latest dishes. Peter went straight into employment after school, but that's not something he'd recommend. 'Had I taken a full-time college course as my parents wanted, I would have made faster progress. There's a shortage of first-class chefs, so many companies are now advertising good salaries, including profit-related pay, to chefs with the right qualifications and experience, though these advantages are more likely to come from the big-name restaurants and hotel chains than small-scale operations'.

C Maria Falcon:
Tour guide

If you enjoy communicating with large groups of people, this is a great job. Maria accompanies groups of holidaymakers on package tours. She knows she plays a central role in ensuring that people enjoy their holiday by providing them with practical support and information throughout the trip. 'It is important to allow people to do what they want, while at the same time making sure everybody is back on the mini-bus by the agreed time. And you must know the history of places you visit really well. Years back, I was embarrassed when a holiday-maker spotted some incorrect details in a commentary I was giving. Since then I've managed to attend regular local history classes to make sure it doesn't happen again.'

D Patrick O'Connor:
Adventure travel guide

Patrick leads trips to exotic locations around the globe, and he's quick to remind us that you need experience in a range of adventurous disciplines. 'People on these holidays are doing potentially dangerous activities, such as kayaking or diving. It's crucial to be able to exercise good judgement in difficult situations and be resourceful when dealing with the emergencies that are bound to arise. Forgetting to give somebody a life-jacket could have serious consequences. This is an increasingly popular career, so educational institutions are beginning to offer a wider range of programmes and qualifications.'

E Connie Ferguson:
Travel Agent

'The recruitment outlook isn't very promising right now in traditional agencies because of the internet, says Connie. 'It's become much easier for people to make their own travel arrangements, though some people still need the advice of a travel professional.' Unlike other tourist jobs, you're based in an office, but you may get the opportunity to visit some destinations to evaluate the facilities on offer. Connie started by working as a reservations clerk in the agency, but the manager soon realised she had the skills to become a travel agent. 'Clients are well informed and expect expert advice. I'm hoping to be able to start my own online travel business soon.'

Part 1

You **must** answer this question. Write your answer in **140 – 190** words in an appropriate style.

1   In your English class you have been discussing the influence of fashion on young people. Now your English teacher has asked you to write an essay.

Write an essay using **all** the notes and giving reasons for your point of view.

Why do many young people want to follow the latest fashion in clothes and hair styles?

Notes

Write about:

1. To be like celebrities they admire

2. To feel accepted in a group

3. .... (your own idea)

Write your **essay**.

Write an answer to **one** of the questions **2 – 4** in this part. Write your answer in **140 – 190** words in an appropriate style.

2   You have seen an advertisement for a part-time job.

> ### Part-time waiters needed
> ### for our international restaurant
>
> You need to:
> - be good at working with people.
> - have some knowledge of foreign languages.
> - be willing to work flexible hours.
>
> Write explaining why you would be suitable for the job to:
>
> **Mr Roy Smith, manager of Carlton Restaurants.**

Write your **letter**.

3   You recently saw this notice in the local newspaper.

> ## Can you write us a review
> ## of a TV soap opera you enjoy?
>
> Tell us about the characters, what makes you keep on watching
> it and if you would recommend it to everyone.
>
> ### The best review wins a smart phone!

Write your **review**.

4   You have received an email from your English-speaking friend Jemma, who is giving a talk about 'Young people and Sport'. Write an email to Jemma, answering her questions.

> How important is sport in the life of young people in your country?
> What are the main sports they do? Is sport part of school or college life? Are there any big sports personalities they look up to?
>
> Thanks for your help!
>
> Jemma

Write your **email**.

You will hear people talking in eight different situations. For questions **1 – 8**, choose the best answer (**A**, **B** or **C**).

1   You hear the weather forecast.
     What will the weather be like on Sunday?
     A   windier than on Saturday
     B   colder than on Saturday
     C   rainier than on Saturday

2   You hear a man talking to his trainer at the gym.
     What is he doing?
     A   apologising for missing a session
     B   explaining how an injury happened
     C   asking to do something less challenging

3   You hear an advertisement.
     What is being advertised?
     A   a shop
     B   a publication
     C   a TV programme

4   You hear part of a soap opera.
     How does the woman feel?
     A   nervous about something
     B   guilty about something
     C   bored by something

5   You hear part of a programme on the subject of fashion.
     What is the presenter's purpose?
     A   to criticise certain attitudes
     B   to complain about something
     C   to recommend something to us

6   You hear a woman talking about the flat she lives in.
     Why is she thinking of selling it?
     A   There's too little storage space.
     B   She's disturbed by street noise.
     C   It's a long way from her place of work.

7   You hear an announcement about a future wildlife event.
     The event will help the protection of wildlife by
     A   raising money.
     B   informing the public.
     C   recruiting volunteers.

8   You hear a couple talking about computer games.
     The man likes them because
     A   they help him to relax after work.
     B   they remind him of his childhood.
     C   they make him more self-confident.

You will hear a student called Jake Townsend giving a presentation about a type of bird called a peacock. For questions **9 – 18**, complete the sentences with a word or short phrase.

The Peacock

Jake mentions that the peacock's tail is said to look similar to a

(9) ....

The original home of the blue peacock is in

(10) ....

Jake explains that peacocks were first kept by people as long as

(11) .... years ago.

Jake describes the peacock's **(12)** ....

as long and thin.

The coloured spots on the peacock's tail are known as

(13) ....

Jake says that the female peahen is mostly

(14) .... in colour.

In English, some people are described as being as

(15) .... as a peacock.

In the wild, peacocks usually live close to

(16) .... in a forest.

Jake tells us that peacocks usually spend time in trees when they want to

(17) ....

At Peacock Paradise in Malaysia, you can see

(18) .... as well as birds.

You will hear five short extracts in which writers are talking about their first novels. For questions **19 – 23**, choose from the list (**A – H**) what each speaker says about writing their first novel. There are three extra letters which you do not need to use.

A   It wasn't as difficult as I thought it would be.

B   My previous style of writing wasn't suitable for it.

Speaker 1	**19**

C   I was determined to make it true to life.

Speaker 2	**20**

D   I believe I should've been paid more to write it.

Speaker 3	**21**

E   It benefited from a course of study I attended.

Speaker 4	**22**

F   I was surprised to be asked to write it.

Speaker 5	**23**

G   I couldn't have written it without the support of my parents.

H   I learnt some of the skills I needed in a previous job.

You will hear an interview with man called David Shaw who is a professional ceramicist, making pottery objects out of clay. For questions **24 – 30**, choose the best answer (**A**, **B** or **C**).

24   What does David say is an absolute requirement for people considering a career in ceramics?

   A   They must feel a passion for it.
   B   They must be physically very fit.
   C   They must have enough patience.

25   David says it took him a long time to

   A   develop his own style.
   B   make his business profitable.
   C   decide to work at ceramics full-time.

26   What does David find most enjoyable about his job?

   A   the fact that the results are unpredictable
   B   the feedback he gets from his customers
   C   the knowledge that he creates useful pieces

27   What does David say he finds particularly difficult?

   A   doing administrative tasks
   B   finding time to research new ideas
   C   finishing his commissions on time

28   What reason does David give for his recent success as a ceramicist?

   A   He's been luckier than other ceramicists.
   B   He's put in more effort than in the past.
   C   He's started to follow certain fashions.

29   How does David feel about the possibility of teaching ceramics?

   A   He feels unprepared for it.
   B   He fears it might distract him.
   C   He's unsure about finding time.

30   David advises people who want a career in ceramics to

   A   talk to established ceramicists.
   B   go to ceramics exhibitions.
   C   attend a ceramics course.

Part 1 (2 minutes)

The examiner will ask you a few questions about yourself and what you think about different things. For example, the examiner might ask you about:

Free time and entertainment

- What outdoor activities do you usually do at weekends?
- Do you ever go to the cinema or theatre? (Tell us what films / plays you like.)
- Do you like going to parties with your friends? (Tell us what you do at a party.)
- How much free time do you have during the week?

Home and family

- Do you like the area where you live? (Why? / Why not?)
- How many people live in your house? (Tell us about them.)
- Do you like preparing your own meals? (Why? / Why not?)
- Do you spend time talking with your family in the evening? (What do you talk about?)

Food and drink

- Do you eat snacks when you're at college / work? (Which?)
- What types of food do you like best? (Why?)
- Do you like having picnics? (Why? / Why not?)
- What do you have for breakfast?

Part 2 (4 minutes)

In this part of the test, I'm going to give each of you two photographs. I'd like you to talk about your photographs on your own for about a minute, and also to answer a question about your partner's photographs.

(Candidate A), it's your turn first. Look at the photographs on page 181. They show **people taking a break**. I'd like you to compare the photographs, and say **why the people needed a break**.

Thank you. (Candidate B), **do you take breaks when you're studying / working?**

Now, (Candidate B), look at your photogrpahs on page 182. They show **people performing in front of an audience**. I'd like you to compare the photographs, and say **how the performers and the audience may be feeling**.

Thank you. (Candidate A), **do you like going to concerts?**

Part 3 (4 minutes)

Now I'd like you to talk about something together for about two minutes. Now look at page183.

I'd like you to imagine that you're giving somebody advice about how to learn a new language. Here are some ways of learning a new language, and a question for you to discuss. First you have some time to look at the task.

Now talk to each other about how useful these ideas are when you're learning a new language.

Thank you. Now you have a minute to decide **which way of learning would be the most difficult for a beginner.**

Part 4 (4 minutes)

Use the following questions in order, as appropriate:

- **Do you think learning a language is different from learning other subjects? (Why? / Why not?)**

- **Do you think your own language is easy or difficult for people from other countries to learn? (Why?)**

- **What's your favourite way of learning difficult things? (Why?)**

- **How important is it for young people to communicate with older people?**

- **Some students say you can learn more in the real world than at college / school. What's your opinion?**

- **Do you think it's a good idea for university students to have part-time jobs? (Why? / Why not?)**

Select any of the following prompts, as appropriate:

- **What do you think?**

- **Do you agree?**

- **And you?**

Thank you. That is the end of the test.

TEST 6

Part I

For questions **1 – 8**, read the text below and decide which answer (**A**, **B**, **C** or **D**) best fits each gap. There is an example at the beginning (**0**).

In the exam, you mark your answers **on a separate answer sheet**.

Example:

0	**A** got	**B** found	**C** reached	**D** received

0	A	B	C	D

My first expedition

When I was about twelve, I **(0)** .... the chance to go to the mountains of western China, looking for rare plants. My Dad's a botanist by **(1)** .... and he was going as assistant to Professor Beall, who was leading the expedition.

It was an important international expedition and my name was **(2)** .... not on the original list of participants. But at the **(3)** .... moment, one of the team broke his ankle and had to **(4)** .... out. It was impossible to get anyone else to go at such **(5)** .... notice, so my dad suggested taking me and the professor agreed.

He obviously began to **(6)** .... doubts, however. On the plane, I remember him saying that he hoped I wasn't going to run around and **(7)** .... on rare specimens! As if I was a little kid. He didn't realise it at the time, but my ambition was to get a photo of a wild panda. And, of course, in the end that's **(8)** .... what I did.

1	**A** work	**B** profession	**C** job	**D** employment
2	**A** completely	**B** definitely	**C** particularly	**D** confidently
3	A late	B final	C last	D end
4	A drop	**B** slip	**C** fall	**D** step
5	A quick	B brief	C fast	D short
6	A have	**B** see	**C** do	**D** feel
7	A tread	B spoil	C squash	D ruin
8	A perfectly	**B** correctly	**C** exactly	**D** accurately

For questions **9 – 16**, read the text below and think of the word which best fits each gap. Use only **one** word in each gap. There is an example at the beginning (**0**).

In the exam, you write your answers **IN CAPITAL LETTERS on a separate answer sheet**.

Example: | **0** | U | P | | | | | | | | | | | | | | | | | | | |

Shopping trolley joins the push for fitness

Although full supermarket trolleys can be quite hard to push **(0)** .... and down the aisles, one store is about to make the task even harder. Next week sees the introduction of **(9)** .... is called Trim Trolley, **(10)** .... is designed to transform the typical forty-minute supermarket visit **(11)** .... a gentle workout.

The Trim Trolley can be set at different levels of resistance, making it harder or easier to push. It's also able to measure both the customer's heart rate **(12)** .... the number of calories burnt through sensors on the handle. Shoppers **(13)** .... thought to burn about 160 calories during a typical forty-minute visit to the supermarket. Pushing the Trim Trolley for that length of time **(14)** .... the resistance level at seven, the average person would burn 280 calories. In **(15)** .... words, the equivalent of a twenty-minute swim. At the highest resistance level, a shopping trip could replace a trip to the gym.

As well as pointing **(16)** .... to people that shopping is a form of exercise, the designers also hope to encourage shoppers to pay more attention to their health generally.

Part 3

For questions **17 – 24**, read the text below. Use the word given in capitals at the end of some of the lines to form a word that fits in the gap **in the same line**. There is an example at the beginning (**0**).

In the exam, you write your answers **IN CAPITAL LETTERS on a separate answer sheet**.

Example: | **0** | T | W | E | N | T | I | E | T | H | | | | | | | | | |

Toy story

In the second half of the **(0)** .... century, toys like model cars and Barbie dolls made the perfect gift for young children. Most of these toys were played with until they fell apart, but others were looked   **TWENTY**

after very **(17)** .... by children who were more interested in building   **CAREFUL**

a **(18)** .... Today such toys are valuable antiques. Barbie made her   **COLLECT**

first **(19)** .... in toy shops over sixty years ago. She's been sold in   **APPEAR**

hundreds of different fashionable **(20)** .... and clothes suitable to a   **FIT**

(21) .... of professions from nurse to astronaut. Today fully-clothed   **VARY**

Barbies sell for hundreds dollars, the most expensive being those in

(22) .... condition, with their original packaging and accessories.   **DAMAGED**

If you're interested in starting a toy collection, another good **(23)** ....   **INVEST**

is Japanese battery-operated robots of the 1960s. Although not very

(24) .... by today's standards, some of these toys are now very rare. If   **IMPRESS**

they are in full working order, they can cost thousands of dollars.

For questions **25 – 30**, complete the second sentence so that it has a similar meaning to the first sentence, using the word given. **Do not change the word given.** You must use between two and five words, including the word given. Here is an example (**0**).

Example:

0   What type of music do you like best?

FAVOURITE

What .... type of music?

The gap can be filled with the words 'is your favourite', so you write:

Example:	0	IS YOUR FAVOURITE

In the exam, you write **only** the missing words **IN CAPITAL LETTERS on a separate answer sheet.**

---

25   Pete hadn't expected to see so many old friends at the party.

SURPRISE

It came .... to see so many old friends at the party.

26   The country's economic problems are less serious than people had been led to believe.

A**S**

The country's economic problems .... people had been led to believe.

27   Adam hadn't finished his homework when Remy arrived.

STILL

Adam .... his homework, when Remy arrived.

28   I think you should complain to your boss.

WERE

If I .... a complaint to my boss.

29   For me, the film was spoilt by the awful soundtrack.

MY

In .... the awful soundtrack which spoilt the film.

30   Toronto has been my home since last March.

LIVING

I have .... last March.

You are going to read an extract from an article about a college. For questions **31 – 36**, choose the answer
(**A**, **B**, **C** or **D**) which you think fits best according to the text.

In the exam, you mark your answers **on a separate answer sheet**.

Assistants to the stars

It stands to reason that a city like Los Angeles, home to so many film stars, would have an Association of Celebrity
Personal Assistants (ACPA). The organisation describes personal assistants as 'multi-tasking', as 'possessing the most
resourceful, creative, insightful, and results-driven abilities.'

When I first got in touch with the organisation's President, he was initially reluctant to talk to me because I was a
journalist. As he sees it, celebrity personal assistants haven't always been treated fairly by the press. But despite this,
and all the hard work and lack of appreciation that can come with this line of work, he explained, the jobs are still
widely sought after. He noted that people regularly travelled great distances to attend a seminar titled 'Becoming a
8 Celebrity Personal Assistant', run by the ACPA. To prove his point, he told me about Dean Johnson. In the coming
weeks, I heard this story from a number of assistants, including Johnson himself, and every time it left me baffled.

The story begins one night with Dean Johnson sitting at home in South Carolina. Johnson is a single, 32-year-old
business executive in charge of marketing and advertising at a sizeable company in the healthcare industry. It is 11
pm and he's looking to unwind in front of the television after a long day's work. A repeat of a talk-show appears on
the screen, and the host introduces her four guests: the celebrity personal assistants for four top Hollywood stars. As
these assistants talk about flying on private jets and attending Hollywood parties, Johnson reaches for a pen and starts
taking notes.

Without wasting another minute, he sets about searching for the contact details of the four assistants on the show. He
soon finds Ron Holder, who works for Whoopi Goldberg. Johnson dials his number, and a minute later Holder picks
up the phone. 'He said I was very lucky to get through,' Johnson told me. 'Apparently, in the three months since he'd
appeared on that talk-show, he'd received about two-hundred calls from people like me, but he was nice enough to chat
for a while.' During their conversation, Holder told Johnson that he should consider attending the ACPA seminar in
Los Angeles.

For someone like Johnson, with almost no connections in the industry, the notion of moving out to Los Angeles
to become a celebrity personal assistant, something he did two months later, was extremely courageous – there's no
denying that. The typical American story of the guy in the remote provinces who falls in love with the glamour of the
silver screen, packs up all his possessions and moves out to Hollywood to become a star is almost a century old. But
Johnson's story offered a new twist: he moved out to Hollywood to become an assistant to a star.

Of the thousands of people who work in Hollywood: agents, lawyers, stylists, publicists, business managers and
others, many hope to rub shoulders with the biggest stars. What's unique about celebrity personal assistants is that
such proximity appears to be the only perk their profession offers. Most describe the bulk of their work as drudgery:
doing laundry, fetching groceries, paying bills. Assistants don't make a fortune by Hollywood standards, especially
given the round-the-clock obligations they often have. What's more, the job is rarely a stepping stone to fame: celebrity
personal assistants are, on average, aged about 38, right in the middle of their professional lives, and most of those I
met described their line of work as a lifelong profession. For them, being an assistant wasn't the means to an end, but
an end in itself.

31 When the writer first contacted him, the ACPA President was

   A   angry about something she'd written.

   B   suspicious of her because of her profession.

   C   surprised that she was interested in his organisation.

   D   pleased that she recognised the importance of assistants.

32 The phrase 'to prove his point' (line **8**) refers to the president's belief that celebrity assistants

   A   enjoy travelling as part of the job.

   B   aren't given the appreciation they deserve.

   C   do jobs that many other people would like to do.

   D   need to do a course before they start looking for work.

33 At the beginning of the story about Dean Johnson, we learn that

   A   he'd turned on the television in order to relax.

   B   he was dissatisfied with the work he was doing.

   C   he'd always wanted to find work in the film industry.

   D   he often watched television programmes about celebrities.

34 What was Dean's immediate reaction to what he saw on the programme?

   A   He wrote down the contact details of the four interviewees.

   B   He decided which of the four interviewees he wanted to talk to.

   C   He started making enquiries about how to find the people on the show.

   D   He read through his notes carefully before getting in touch with anyone.

35 In the fifth paragraph, the writer suggests that Dean Johnson

   A   never achieved his aim of becoming a personal assistant.

   B   was brave to go and look for a new career in Los Angeles.

   C   lived to regret his decision to give up everything in his old life.

   D   really wanted to become a star rather than a personal assistant.

36 In the final paragraph, we learn that celebrity assistants

   A   often move into other aspects of the film industry.

   B   find the job too demanding as they get older.

   C   are relatively well paid for the work they do.

   D   tend to see the job as their career goal.

You are going to read an article. Six sentences have been removed from the article. Choose from the sentences **A – G** the one which fits each gap (**37 – 42**). There is one extra sentence you do not need to use.

In the exam, you mark your answers **on a separate answer sheet**.

Cayman Brac and Little Cayman

Few destinations feel further from life in the 21st century than Cayman Brac and Little Cayman – the less well-known sister islands of Grand Cayman in the Caribbean. A stay on one – or both – is the perfect tonic for anyone who is tired, stressed and in need of a proper break.

It's not all about relaxing in the sun, though, and lovers of the outdoors will be in their element | **37** | The Cayman Islands form one of the world's top three dive destinations and divers flock from all corners of the world to explore their waters. The range of marine life is so phenomenal that a large part of the *The Blue Planet* television series was filmed here. Those seeking a once-in-a-lifetime underwater experience can stop in the Cayman Islands and book a trip in a submarine that takes them down three-hundred metres to discover weird and wonderful creatures rarely seen nearer the surface. More people have travelled in space than have been down this far into the depths of the sea.

Although Cayman Brac and Little Cayman have fundamental similarities, they are quite different in geography and atmosphere. Little Cayman is not really built up apart from a few small hotels, a couple of very good local restaurants and a quirky museum. | **38** |

It goes without saying that the diving around Little Cayman is excellent. An extra draw is the coral reef called the Bloody Bay Wall. | **39** | Here amid the wall's colourful coral, divers will find butterfly fish, angelfish and bonefish. If they are lucky, a turtle or two will swim lazily past. Even if you don't dive, there is so much to see just below the surface that snorkelling is fascinating enough.

But Little Cayman is not just about the sea. | **40** | Its wonderfully varied natural environment is best seen by exploring the island by bike. All in all, Little Cayman has a unique appeal. Who could fail to be charmed by an island where the fire engine is bigger than the airport building, and where iguanas have right of way on the road?

Cayman Brac, although not much bigger, is quite different. | **41** | The locals are friendly people who love to chat, each one with their own fascinating story to tell. The landscape in Cayman Brac is also surprisingly hilly, with dense woodland, secret caves and a vertical cliff that rises fifty metres on the east side of the island.

This diverse scenery has created a unique natural habitat that can be explored by walking the eight miles of public footpaths and hiking trails. Cayman Brac is a natural stopping-off point for migrating birds. | **42** | Great fishing opportunities and a selection of excellent hotels complete the picture.

Whether you want to explore the underwater world or keep your head above water, a holiday on either Cayman Brac or Little Cayman is guaranteed to leave you feeling as good as new. These laid-back islands will capture your imagination like few other places on earth ever could.

A   It starts at seven metres deep and suddenly plunges to a staggering two-thousand metres.

B   As well as these visitors, it is also home to nearly two hundred resident species, including an endangered parrot.

C   This should not be a problem as there are now at least two airlines which fly to the islands regularly.

D   Back on land, there is more nature to be discovered.

E   They will love the walking and the cycling, and in particular the wonderful opportunities for diving and snorkelling.

F   It is this lack of development that attracts visitors to its shores year after year.

G   With roughly 1,600 inhabitants to its neighbour's 120, it is much livelier.

Part 7

You are going to read an article about bookshop managers. For questions **43 – 52,** choose from the graduates **(A – D)**. The graduates may be chosen more than once.

In the exam, you mark your answers **on a separate answer sheet**.

Which bookshop manager …

feels the shop has another function as well as selling books? | 43 |

believes customers are attracted by the way the books are displayed? | 44 |

spent some time finding out about the area before opening the shop? | 45 |

is critical of the customer service offered by some bookshops? | 46 |

explains why a previous job was given up? | 47 |

is proud of the shop's stock of books for the very young? | 48 |

mentions a link between customers' occupations and their choice of books? | 49 |

has some knowledge about the content of all the books on sale? | 50 |

is able to organise cultural events on the premises? | 51 |

mentions the fact that local people prefer the shop to larger ones? | 52 |

The bestsellers

Dan Branson visits four successful bookshop managers

A   Mandy Stocks: Saville Books

This shop is small and beautiful and it doesn't stock best-sellers, preferring to promote less well-known young authors. The children's section demonstrates the difference in philosophy between this and most other shops. 'We carry a vast range of books that reflect reality,' says Mandy. 'The vast majority of bookshops don't show children the world the way it is.' You could question the need to have games and so many other products in a bookshop, but Mandy says it would be incomplete without them. 'This shop's also an information centre,' she says. There are some much bigger bookshops in the area, but Mandy says buyers from the area are loyal and realise that hers offers them a better service. Earlier this month, Saville Books was named Bookseller of the Year in recognition of the effort and imagination that Mandy has put into the shop.

B   Andrew Welson: Lonestar Bookshop

Andrew is a very experienced bookseller. He ran a second-hand bookshop for several years until the need to increase his income made him apply for a position as manager of Lonestar. 'There's a huge disparity in quality among large bookshops,' he says. 'The best are very good, but others aren't, because the people at the face of helping the customer don't feel they're valued and the managers tend not to have a history of bookselling. You need to be passionate about the things you're selling.' The shop's modern and stylish. 'We only have a certain amount of space and what we're trying to do is stock the kind of books that our customers – mostly university students and young professionals – come to this shop for. But I also stock the popular books everyone's talking about.' Andrew gives a lot of attention to making his shop window eye-catching and interesting. 'It is incredibly important,' he says.

C   Jane Harvard: Brunswick Bookshop

Jane opened the Brunswick Bookshop last November, and it's the sort of place that captivates you as soon you go through the door. Jane's been in bookselling, at three different shops, for fifteen years. Last year, she decided to take the plunge and set up on her own. She was planning to open a shop in a fashionable part of the city, but then discovered a less well-off market district. 'The moment I saw it I knew it was right because it's a community street. I came and sat in the cafés and listened to conversations to see what kind of people lived here. They were well-educated but didn't necessarily have much money.' Everything in her shop Jane wants to read herself. 'Obviously you don't have time to read them all, but I've got a pretty good idea of what's in most of them,' she says.

D   James Darry: Darry Books

Darry Books is light, airy, modern and welcoming. It's got a strong children's section, a coffee bar, and also a space upstairs for author talks and presentations of new books. James is a former school head and left his job to start the bookshop. Why did he do it? 'I was having a conversation with a colleague one day, about what we could've done instead of teaching, and I said I'd have had a bookshop. A year later, I opened this shop, but it hasn't been easy. The competition from larger chains is horrendous, so I offer lots of discounts.' James had four full-time employees. 'We treat bookselling as a proper career and the staff are motivated, interested and well paid. The book trade's changing fast and we have to change with it, by offering customers that special personal touch.'

Part I

You **must** answer this question. Write your answer in **140 – 190** words in an appropriate style.

1   In your English class you have been discussing the advantages and disadvantages of living in the city or in the countryside. Now your English teacher has asked you to write an essay.

Write an essay using all the notes and giving reasons for your point of view.

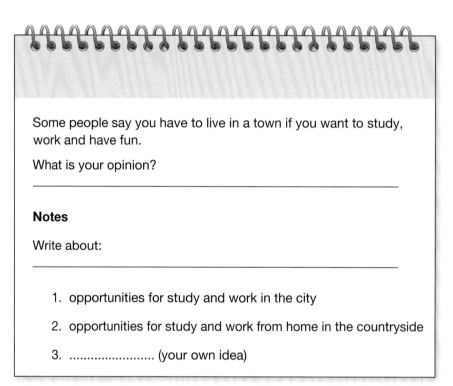

Some people say you have to live in a town if you want to study, work and have fun.

What is your opinion?

Notes

Write about:

1. opportunities for study and work in the city

2. opportunities for study and work from home in the countryside

3. .... (your own idea)

Write your **essay**.

Write an answer to **one** of the questions **2 – 4** in this part. Write your answer in **140 – 190** words in an appropriate style.

2   You have seen this advertisement and you want to apply.

Brassbolt TV Studios
Do you want a four-week work experience placement in our TV studios?

Join one of these teams:
- **Sports news presenters**
- **Make-up artists**
- **Camera operators**

Write to **Tim Beal**, **recruitment manager**, saying which team you'd like to join and why; whether you have any experience; when you'd be able to start and how he can contact you.

Write your **letter**.

3   A pop band recently gave a concert in the college where you study. This announcement has appeared in the college website.

Write a review of the concert!

What did you think of the college concert? Write a review for the college website. Include your opinion about the choice of songs, the performers and say whether you think the college hall was a suitable venue.

The best review will be published!

Write your **review**.

4   Your local library has a small amount of money to spend on materials that would be useful for students in the area. You've been asked to write a report for the chief librarian saying whether the money should be spent on books, magazines or computer equipment.

Write your **report**.

Part I

You will hear people talking in eight different situations. For questions **1 – 8**, choose the best answer (**A**, **B** or **C**).

1   You hear part of a talk by a man who works for a tourist company.
     What is his role in the company?
     A   He trains the guides.
     B   He chooses the destinations.
     C   He designs the advertisements.

2   You overhear two people talking about a film.
     Why didn't the man enjoy it?
     A   He was distracted by noise.
     B   His seat was uncomfortable.
     C   The sound volume was too low.

3   You hear a woman talking about running in a marathon.
     Why did she decide to run?
     A   She knew it would be good for her level of fitness.
     B   She'd been wanting to do it since her schooldays.
     C   She was too embarrassed to refuse to do it.

4   You hear a man talking about an antique calculator.
     What does he say about it?
     A   It's just been stolen.
     B   It's just been found.
     C   It's just been sold.

5   You hear a politician talking about facilities for the young in her area.
     In her opinion, what is needed?
     A   a library
     B   a leisure centre
     C   an internet café

6   You overhear a woman talking about a full-time job in a theatre.
     She decided not to apply for it because
     A   she was used to working part time.
     B   she would have had to work evenings.
     C   she felt she lacked the right qualifications.

7   You hear a comedian talking about the 'laughter workshops' he organises.
     He wants to teach the participants how to
     A   make friends more easily.
     B   become more self-confident.
     C   help others overcome problems.

8   You hear a woman talking about learning to fly a plane.
     How did she feel during her first lesson?
     A   alarmed by the way the plane moved
     B   relieved that it seemed relatively easy
     C   confused by the instructor's comments

You will hear a man called Darren Howarth giving a presentation about his work as what's called a carbon coach. For questions **9 – 18**, complete the sentences with a word or short phrase.

The carbon coach

As a carbon coach, Darren works full-time as a

(9) .... with various clients.

Darren trained to be an **(10)** ....

before becoming a carbon coach.

When assessing a family's carbon footprint, Darren begins by looking at their

(11) ....

Darren uses something called a **(12)** ....

to see how much electricity things use.

Darren points out that **(13)** ....

can help pay for roof insulation.

Darren feels that using **(14)** ....

of the old type is the worst waste of energy he sees.

Darren helped to reduce a band's carbon footprint at

(15) .... as well as on its recordings.

Darren mentions a type of green home called an

(16) ....

The new green home uses both the sun and

(17) .... to produce electricity.

Darren suggests buying a **(18)** .... ,

which gives more information about the new green home.

You will hear five short extracts in which people are talking about the sport of hillwalking. For questions **19 – 23**, choose from the list (**A – H**) the reason each person gives for taking up the sport. There are three extra letters which you do not need to use.

A   Other sports had failed to improve my fitness.

B   I had plans to do some serious climbing later on.

Speaker 1   **19**

C   My ambition was to lead hillwalking groups.

Speaker 2   **20**

D   I was hoping it would solve a health problem I had.

Speaker 3   **21**

E   I wanted to be able to enjoy hillwalking with other people.

Speaker 4   **22**

F   I realised it would be more fun than other sporting activities.

Speaker 5   **23**

G   My trainer advised me to give it a try.

H   I heard it was a good way of making new friends.

You will hear an interview with a woman called Jennie Thorpe, who is a trapeze artist in a circus. For questions **24 – 30**, choose the best answer (**A**, **B** or **C**).

24   Jennie got her present job when her manager saw her performing at

    A   a gymnastics competition.

    B   a circus school.

    C   a ballet show.

25   Why does Jennie feel a need to practise just after the end of a show?

    A   She's able to do more difficult things then.

    B   She's too tense to be able to relax immediately.

    C   She's able to sleep better afterwards.

26   What does Jennie say about earning a living as a trapeze artist?

    A   It's hard if you have no contract.

    B   It's unlikely after a certain age.

    C   It's difficult for most performers.

27   According to Jennie, what distinguishes great trapeze artists from the rest?

    A   They have the lightest bodies.

    B   They perform without a safety net.

    C   They have an ability to keep calm.

28   What does Jennie find the most difficult thing to get used to?

    A   having to get up early every day

    B   damaging her hands on the trapeze

    C   feeling pain in her muscles

29   In Jennie's opinion, circus skills have helped some school students by

    A   making them physically stronger.

    B   increasing their ability to study.

    C   improving their social interaction.

30   What does Jennie want to do next?

    A   do a training course

    B   get a teaching job

    C   open a circus school

Part 1 (2 minutes)

The examiner will ask you a few questions about yourself and what you think about different things. For example, the examiner might ask you about:

Fitness and sport

* Do you do any sport in your spare time? (Why? / Why not?)
* Is it difficult to find the time to get enough exercise (Why? / Why not?)
* What types of food do you think are really good for you? (Why?)
* Is there a sports club in the area where you live? (Tell us about it.)

Holidays and travel

* Have you been on holiday recently? (Tell us about it.)
* What's your favourite means of transport when you go on holiday? (Why?)
* Do you think it's important to plan a trip carefully? (Why? / Why not?)
* Do you prefer to have short breaks or long holidays? (Why?)

Celebrations and special occasions

* Do you and your friends usually give each other birthday presents? (Why? / Why not?)
* What special occasions do people in your country celebrate most?
* What food and drink would you and your friends have at a party?
* Do people in your country like to celebrate success at big sports events? (How?)

Part 2 (4 minutes)

I'm going to give each of you two photographs. I'd like you to talk about your photographs on your own for about a minute, and also to answer a question about your partner's photographs.

(Candidate A), it's your turn first. Look at the photographs on page 184. They show **people communicating in different ways**. I'd like you to compare the photographs, and say **how necessary it is for the people to communicate in these ways**.

Thank you. *(Candidate B)*, **do you use your phone a lot?**

Now, *(Candidate B)*, look at your photogrpahs on page 185. They show **people taking part in competitions**. I'd like you to compare the photographs, and say **how the people may be feeling**.

Thank you. *(Candidate A)*, **do you like competitions?**

Part 3 (4 minutes)

Now I'd like you to talk about something together for about two minutes. Now look at page 186.

I'd like you to imagine that a college / school is planning to invite people with interesting jobs to come and tell students about their work. Here are some jobs they are thinking of, and a question for you to discuss. First you have some time to look at the task.

Now talk to each other about **how difficult or easy it might be to do these jobs.**

Thank you. Now you have a minute to decide **which two questions you would ask all the speakers.**

Part 4 (4 minutes)

Use the following questions in order, as appropriate:

- **Do you think having visitors like this in schools is a good idea? (Why? / Why not?)**
- **How would you feel if you had to work in the evening or at weekends?**
- **Some young people do volunteer work in other countries. Do you think it's a good idea? (Why? / Why not?)**
- **Do you think some people earn too much money? (Why? / Why not?)**
- **Some young people go into the same careers as their parents. Do you think this is a good idea? (Why? / Why not?)**
- **What would be your ideal job? (Why?)**

Select any of the following prompts, as appropriate:

- **What do you think?**
- **Do you agree?**
- **And you?**

Thank you. That is the end of the test.

TEST 7

For questions **1 – 8**, read the text below and decide which answer (**A, B, C** or **D**) best fits each gap. There is an example at the beginning (**0**).

In the exam, you mark your answers **on a separate answer sheet**.

Example:

| 0 | **A** item | **B** object | **C** matter | **D** aspect |

0	A	B	C	D
	▬	▭	▭	▭

Baseball caps

Today, the baseball cap is a very well-known (**0**) .... of clothing, even to people who are (**1**) .... with the game of baseball. The cap was invented over a century ago as a way of (**2**) .... the sun out of baseball players' eyes, but soon became fashionable off the field too.

By the 1940s, teams were beginning to have their logos sewn on to the caps they wore during matches. The (**3**) .... thing for fans to do was to wear these too. Sales of caps went through the roof as the idea of showing (**4**) .... to their college team in this way (**5**) .... on amongst students...

By the late 1970s, new technology (**6**) .... that it was possible to embroider images of things like animals and flags onto caps (**7**) .... of just names and numbers. The caps now became fashionable once again, (**8**) .... thanks to hip-hop music bands who wore them on stage.

1	**A** uninterested	**B** unfamiliar	**C** unrelated	**D** uninformed
2	**A** taking	**B** keeping	**C** minding	**D** protecting
3	**A** obvious	**B** apparent	**C** certain	**D** evident
4	**A** following	**B** trust	**C** support	**D** loyalty
5	**A** caught	**B** picked	**C** joined	**D** chose
6	**A** allowed	**B** made	**C** caused	**D** meant
7	**A** replace	**B** alternative	**C** instead	**D** preference
8	**A** greatly	**B** largely	**C** fully	**D** widely

For questions **9 – 16**, read the text below and think of the word which best fits each gap. Use only **one** word in each gap. There is an example at the beginning (**0**).

In the exam, you write your answers **IN CAPITAL LETTERS on a separate answer sheet**.

Example: | 0 | | W | E | R | E | | | | | | | | | | | | | | | |

Unemployed elephants

In Thailand, the elephant has always played an important economic and cultural role, and until the end of the twentieth century the animals **(0)** .... employed in the forestry industry, to do heavy lifting work.

In recent years, **(9)** .... , the forestry industry in Thailand has been **(10)** .... decline, partly because people there want to conserve the forests **(11)** .... than cut them down. This means there are now a large number of unemployed elephants which are in **(12)** .... of a new life.

The government-run Elephant Conservation Centre near Chiang Mai tries to help some of these animals. It provides around one hundred of them **(13)** .... a home. What's more, it's now regarded **(14)** .... the best place in the world to learn the skills of elephant care. The centre also attracts large numbers of tourists **(15)** .... come to see the animals. Everyone's favourite activity is bath time in the river, and the elephants obviously enjoy it just as **(16)** .... as their visitors.

For questions **17 – 24**, read the text below. Use the word given in capitals at the end of some of the lines to form a word that fits in the gap **in the same line**. There is an example at the beginning (**0**).

In the exam, you write your answers **IN CAPITAL LETTERS on a separate answer sheet**.

Example: | 0 | F | A | V | O | U | R | I | T | E | | | | | | | | |

Bananas

If asked to name their **(0)** .... fruit, many people would	**FAVOUR**
say it was the banana. And if asked why, they would tell	
you that it was because it is a **(17)** .... food which is both	**NATURE**
(18) .... and full of energy.	**TASTE**
The banana needs hot and damp conditions for **(19)**	**SUCCESS**
growth such as those found in the **(20)** .... lowlands of	**COAST**
tropical areas. Even so, the plants are **(21)** .... attacked	**CONSTANT**
by a number of diseases which seriously threaten to destroy	
the fruit if it is left **(22)** .... That's why, of all the world's	**PROTECT**
food crops, the banana probably needs the highest level of	
chemical **(23)**	**TREAT**
Bananas are produced in enormous plantations, which	
supply a highly developed shipping and **(24)** .... network	**DISTRIBUTE**
that ensures each fruit reaches its point of sale, often on the	
other side of the world, just twelve or so days after being cut	
from the tree.	

For questions **25 – 30**, complete the second sentence so that it has a similar meaning to the first sentence, using the word given. **Do not change the word given.** You must use between **two** and **five** words, including the word given. Here is an example (**0**).

Example:

0   What type of music do you like best?

   Is your FAVOURITE

   What .... type of music?

The gap can be filled with the words 'is your favourite', so you write:

Example: | **0** | *IS YOUR FAVOURITE*

In the exam, you write **only** the missing words **IN CAPITAL LETTERS on a separate answer sheet.**

---

25   Roberta no longer tries to understand her son's computer games.

   GIVEN

   Roberta has .... to understand her son's computer games.

26   When he was at college, Ali played tennis a lot.

   USED

   Ali .... of tennis when he was at college.

27   Verna didn't learn to swim until she was sixteen years old.

   ABLE

   Verna .... until she was sixteen years old.

28   'Check that your computer is turned off before you go out,' said Carl's mother.

   SURE

   Carl's mother told .... his computer was turned off before he went out.

29   There was no sugar left at all in the supermarket.

   RUN

   The supermarket had .... sugar completely.

30   Sandra doesn't want anyone to know that she is moving house.

   TRYING

   Sandra .... the fact that she is moving house a secret.

You are going to read an extract from a magazine article about a language course. For questions **31 – 36**, choose the answer (**A, B, C** or **D**) which you think fits best according to the text.

In the exam, you mark your answers **on a separate answer sheet**.

I was on holiday in Greece with my parents and my brother Joe. It was all very beautiful and mostly I was enjoying myself, but my family were getting on my nerves. They told me things all the time. They were usually interesting things, but I got really fed up with the way they always knew stuff I didn't. They told me stories from Greek myths; they showed me how olives and lemons grow; they taught me how to eat an artichoke. I can't think of anything they didn't tell me. I remember sitting outside a café on the beach eating honey cake
6 and thinking that my head was so full it didn't have enough room for a single extra fact or figure.

Then my father suggested visiting a tiny rocky island we could see, so we went down to the water's edge where the boats were moored, and my father talked with two fishermen. An older one only spoke Greek, but his son, Stefanos, spoke English. Although he was really friendly and helpful, when my father asked about a trip to the island, he shook his head and said it was only a rock and no one went there. My mother said we'd like to have a picnic on it, but Stefanos said that was out of the question because there were a lot of submerged rocks
12 around it, which made landing too risky. But to make up for it he offered to take us night fishing.

He took us out at sunset, and it was beautiful. There were big lamps fixed to the boat and when Stefanos lit them they made a soft hissing sound. My mother was watching the land, where thousands of tiny fireflies were flickering among the trees. But I was looking in the other direction because I'd seen something amazing – a silver seal. My father said he wasn't sure if there were seals in Greece and my mother said there definitely wouldn't be silver ones. I think Joe believed me, but by the time he looked where I was pointing, it had gone – and even I was beginning to wonder if I'd imagined it.

Stefanos didn't say anything. He stopped rowing and lowered a net into the water, saying that we might get fish there. He said they came to the light. And then I saw it again, moving towards us, trailing shimmering streaks through the water. It looked completely magical. Joe shouted out that I was right, it was a seal. It submerged again and my father explained to us that it wasn't really silver; it was just that there was phosphorescence in the water. I expect he told us all about the microscopic sea creatures that form phosphorescence, but I didn't listen. Stefanos said the seals were rare and shy, but I just wanted to know where mine had gone.

After that I couldn't pay attention to anything else. But there was no sign of the seal. But Stefanos put my mind at rest, explaining that seals stay underwater for a long time. Perhaps I hadn't seen the last of my seal after all.

31 In the first paragraph, we learn that the writer

    A   was finding her family irritating.

    B   was bored by all the things she was being told.

    C   was feeling unsure of herself in unfamiliar surroundings.

    D   was having trouble remembering all the things she'd learnt.

32 The word 'it' in line **6** refers to

    A   the writer's head.

    B   a room in the café.

    C   a single piece of information.

    D   something the writer was eating.

33 Why did the family decide not to visit the island?

    A   They discovered that nobody was allowed to go there.

    B   There wasn't a suitable place for a picnic there.

    C   The fishermen had no time to take them there.

    D   It wasn't safe to take a boat out there.

34 The phrase 'to make up for it' in line **12** suggests that Stefanos

    A   realised that the writer's mother didn't believe him.

    B   was aware that the family was disappointed.

    C   knew that the family enjoyed going fishing.

    D   was sorry that he'd appeared unfriendly.

35 When the writer first noticed a seal in the water,

    A   all of her family thought she had imagined it.

    B   it was too dark to see what colour it was.

    C   she heard it before she actually saw it.

    D   nobody else caught sight of it.

36 How did the writer feel after the seal's second appearance?

    A   pleased that her brother had been proved wrong

    B   impressed to hear that she'd seen a rare animal

    C   unable to concentrate on any other activities

    D   unconvinced by the explanation of its colour

Part 6

You are going to read an article about the use of robots. Six sentences have been removed from the article. Choose from the sentences **A – G** the one which fits each gap (**37 – 42**). There is one extra sentence you do not need to use.

In the exam, you mark your answers **on a separate answer sheet**.

Making special effects for the film *The Fountain*

'I created outer space for Hollywood – in a Pyrex dish', says **Chris Parks**

I first met the director, Darren Aronofsky, some years ago when he asked me to work on his film, *The Fountain*. He'd been all set to shoot it two years earlier, but the main actor he'd lined up pulled out at the last minute. No star meant no movie, and the studio had pulled the plug. But Darren was intent on resurrecting the film, and one day he called my studio to say he'd managed to persuade the studio to fund a different version, and the film was back on again. **37**

We'd produced some sample special effects for the original project, which we thought had been wasted effort. **38** Our effects work would now be central to a re-imagined version. Darren had also liked the optical effects my father had done on the original Superman movies, and he was soon visiting us again in England to set out his vision for this new film.

39 He was looking for something more lifelike, something with as little computer-generated imagery (CGI) as possible, something more real. He felt the CGI vision of space had become the standard that most directors were unwilling to challenge. With CGI, everything has to be so precise and defined, so it doesn't allow for any of the unpredictability that we see in the world. Digital imagery is also constantly improving, so what looked mind-blowing a year or two ago may look dated now.

It was with all this in mind that Darren approached us. Our background in micro-photography appealed to Darren – he thought it would enable us to capture the sort of cosmos he was seeking. My father had made a career out of close-up shooting of very small things – such as marine plankton in the Great Barrier Reef or butterflies in Borneo. **40**

I'd start with a small Pyrex dish of clear liquids – this is my canvas, albeit a three-dimensional, constantly moving one. **41** I use fluids that, through their mutual reaction, cause a microscopic movement or flow, which I then capture in extreme close-up on moving film and in still photographs.

We recreated a meteor storm, for example, by mixing individual specks of curry powder with drops of alcohol and then capturing on film the resulting explosion. And we were able to recreate the surface of the sun using a combination of iodine, water, colourings and other liquids. **42** When transferred to the big screen, that conveys the sun's awesome, galactic power.

A A major chunk of *The Fountain* would be set in outer space, and Darren was determined to avoid the unrealistic 'Star Wars' depictions of space.

B When brought together in the right way, they have a movement, texture and reddy-orange colour that's indistinguishable from the real solar surface.

C For somebody used to Hollywood's glamour, I don't know quite what he made of our working environment.

D There was one condition, though, which was that my father, Peter, and I did the special effects.

E We decided to use this method we were so good at, along with a technique called 'fluid painting'.

F I'd then add single drops of paint, inks and dyes, and start to mix the liquids with my tiny brushes, needles and miniature palette knives.

G Little did we know that, a few years later, this unused material would be unearthed and would prove the crucial factor in Warner Bros agreeing to re-launch the film.

You are going to read an article about students who took gap years. For questions **43 – 52**, choose from the graduates (**A – D**). The graduates may be chosen more than once.

In the exam, you mark your answers **on a separate answer sheet**.

Which student …

was happy to find a gap year activity which suited them perfectly?	**43**
noticed how other people had been changed by a gap year experience?	**44**
had to find ways of earning money before going on a gap year trip?	**45**
mentions not being expected to have outstanding skills in one area?	**46**
realised that they lacked knowledge and skills in certain areas?	**47**
believes gap year experience looks good on a job application?	**48**
advises people against going on a gap year trip alone?	**49**
was determined not to waste the time spent on a gap year?	**50**
took somebody's advice on how to record events during a gap year?	**51**
was only able to spend half the year on the main activity?	**52**

The 'Gap Year': experiencing new sights, climates and cultures

A   Richard Olmos

When I left school, I felt it was time to do something different before going to university. I wanted to fill my gap year with project activities and gain new skills. I knew there would be real benefits in doing it, provided I used the time to maximum advantage. I spent four months on a teaching project in Ghana before travelling through Africa. Working with people who came from such a different world to me really opened my mind. When I started my degree back home, I could tell who had been on a gap year and who hadn't. Those who had were very obviously more mature. My advice to other gap year students is to evaluate what you've learnt afterwards and mention it when writing to prospective employers, because you don't want your good work to be dismissed as simply a 'holiday'.

B   John Saffron

Believe it or not, it's possible to choose to spend a gap year focusing on sports. I live in London, I'm mad about football, so when I read in a magazine about a new gap year scheme a major football club was organising, I jumped at the chance of applying. Basically I spent four months working with children who were underperforming in Maths and IT in a London school, encouraging them to get their work done by giving them a football session in the afternoons. At the same time, I was given the opportunity of taking a course in coaching. Then I spent some time doing the same thing in a school in Australia. The thing is you don't have to be brilliant at the sport. It's more important to have enthusiasm and good communication skills – you need to show you have them when they interview you.

C   Louisa Powell

When you go on a gap year, you often have to cover your own expenses, you are a self-funding volunteer, and as I am a poor student, I had to divide my gap year into two blocks – a 'saving' block then an 'experiencing' block. As soon as my exams were over, I frantically applied for jobs and more jobs. As well as working in an office, I squeezed in an extra few hours working in a café to save up for my gap year. I then spent six months working in one of South Africa's wildlife conservation projects. From my gap year I learned that I couldn't cook and that I was completely ignorant about anything that wasn't 'western'. Furthermore, I came to realise that I wasn't nearly as clever as I thought I was.

D   Frank Holler

A representative from an organisation that helps students find their ideal gap year placement came to our school. She said it was a good idea to spend a minimum of six months in one place. Another important thing she stressed was the need to know exactly how you're going to write up all your activities in a gap year. She suggested keeping a journal, which I did. I needed to raise funds for my gap year, and I did it by asking lots of people for small donations. I spent my gap year working as a language assistant in English language classes in Japan. I went to some ordinary classes to improve my Japanese and get to know other students. It was a great way to experience a different culture, and the best way to learn Japanese. After my gap year, everyone said I seemed more worldly. But I'd recommend going with somebody else, as it can be quite isolating if you're on your own.

Part 1

You **must** answer this question. Write your answer in **140 – 190** words in an appropriate style.

1   In your English class you have been discussing what a healthy lifestyle is and what busy young people can do to make sure they have one. Now your English teacher has asked you to write an essay.

Write an essay using **all** the notes and giving reasons for your point of view.

Some people say it's impossible to have a healthy lifestyle when you're studying or working hard. What is your opinion?

Notes

Write about:

1. achieving a good work/leisure balance

2. finding the time to cook healthy food

3. .... (your own idea)

Write your **essay**.

Write an answer to **one** of the questions **2 – 4** in this part. Write your answer in **140 – 190** words in an appropriate style.

2   This is part of an email you've received from your English-speaking friend:

> I heard that you're planning to take a year off to travel after you leave school. I may want to do the same! Can you tell me if you've found useful information and what kind of trip you want to do? I'd like to do some voluntary work, but I don't know what.
> Please write soon,
>
> Vicky

Write your **email**.

3   You recently saw this notice in your college magazine.

Write a review for us!

Have you visited a museum lately? If so, could you write a review of your visit for the college magazine? Include information about the exhibits, the information available and the facilities, and say whether you would recommend the museum to other students.

*The best reviews will receive a **book token as a prize**.*

Write your **review**.

4   You have seen this advertisement and you want to apply.

SENFORD COLLEGE
Do you want to learn how to organise events professionally?

We have courses on how to organise:
parties
sports events
music and entertainment events
holidays and tours

Write to **Sandra Wright**, **Course Manager**, saying which course you want to attend and why, and whether you have any previous experience of organising an event.

Write your **letter.**

Part I

You will hear people talking in eight different situations. For questions **1 – 8**, choose the best answer (**A**, **B** or **C**).

1   You hear a woman talking about a folk music festival.
     What did she dislike about it?
     A   the way it was organised
     B   some of the performances
     C   the behaviour of the audience

2   You hear a TV presenter talking about a programme that's on later tonight.
     What type of programme is it?
     A   a music programme
     B   a documentary
     C   a chat show

3   You overhear a teacher talking on the phone.
     Who is she talking to?
     A   a colleague
     B   a student
     C   a parent

4   You hear a man talking about pollution.
     He thinks people need to know more about
     A   the proposed solutions.
     B   the effects on humans.
     C   the animals at risk.

5   You hear part of an interview with a sportsman.
     What is his sport?
     A   cycling
     B   football
     C   athletics

6   On a phone-in consumer programme, you hear a call from a listener.
     What is she doing?
     A   making an apology
     B   asking for advice
     C   justifying her behaviour

7   You hear two students discussing the issue of zoos.
     They agree about the need to
     A   conserve rare species of animals.
     B   attract the public to zoos.
     C   keep some zoos open.

8   You hear the beginning of a programme.
     What are the presenters going to visit today?
     A   a nature reserve
     B   an interesting shop
     C   an rather unusual house

You will hear a woman called Mara Barnes talking about the sport of surfing. For questions **9 – 18**, complete the sentences with a word or short phrase.

Mara Barnes: Surfer

Mara says she enjoys feeling totally **(9)** ....

after her two daily summer training sessions.

Out of the water, Mara uses both **(10)** ....

and stretching as a way of keeping fit.

During swimming sessions, Mara aims to do her target distance in under

(11) .... minutes.

Mara's worse injury happened when her **(12)** ....

was broken by her surfboard.

Mara mentions that water **(13)** ....

is less of a problem in her area than it used to be.

Mara used to suffer from sore **(14)** ....

when she went surfing.

The largest wave Mara has ever surfed was at a place called

(15) .... in Hawaii.

Mara says that she no longer eats either **(16)** .... or ....

Mara says she felt a lot better after only eating

(17) .... for a fortnight.

If she feels too nervous before a competition, Mara likes to play

(18) ....

Part 3

You will hear five short extracts in which company directors are talking about recruiting new members of staff. For questions **19 – 23**, choose from the list **(A – H)** what each speaker looks for most when employing a new member of staff. There are three extra letters which you do not need to use.

A   experience in basic office duties

B   an ability to work well in a team

C   an understanding of the latest technology

D   excellent communication skills

E   a willingness to work overtime if asked

F   the initiative to solve problems

G   prestigious academic qualifications

H   the ability to be well-organised

Speaker 1   **19**

Speaker 2   **20**

Speaker 3   **21**

Speaker 4   **22**

Speaker 5   **23**

You will hear an interview with a man called Graham Malley, who's a chef and a restaurant owner. For questions **24 – 30**, choose the best answer (**A**, **B** or **C**).

24   Why did Graham choose to open a restaurant in a small town?

    A   It was ideal for a relaxed life.

    B   He owned a property there.

    C   It was where his family lived.

25   For Graham, the only problem of having a restaurant in a small town is that

    A   tourists don't come in large numbers.

    B   it's difficult to keep qualified staff.

    C   there are fewer ingredients available.

26   What does Graham regard as the most valuable experience during his time at college?

    A   learning to produce business plans

    B   watching professional chefs at work

    C   having to prepare his own meals

27   According to Graham, which skill distinguishes great chefs from others?

    A   Their dishes are always top quality.

    B   They constantly create new recipes.

    C   They are able to inspire their staff.

28   Graham says that recently qualified cooks often

    A   lack practical skills for the job.

    B   have unrealistic expectations.

    C   are poorly paid for their efforts.

29   In what way has Graham changed over the years?

    A   His energy levels have decreased.

    B   He has become more pessimistic.

    C   Financial matters trouble him less.

30   What does Graham see himself doing in ten years' time?

    A   Running a successful restaurant abroad.

    B   Travelling widely to see the world.

    C   Living a quiet life in a different country.

Part 1 (2 minutes)

The examiner will ask you a few questions about yourself and what you think about different things. For example, the examiner might ask you about:

Everyday life

- How big is your family? (Tell us about it.)
- Do you have to get up very early every day? (Why? / Why not?)
- Where is the best place to go if you want to read in your house? (Why?)
- Who does the cooking in your house? (Tell us about the meals you enjoy.)

Free time and entertainment

- Do you like watching horror films? (Why? / Why not?)
- What do you do when you go out in the evening with friends?
- Do you ever go for long walks? (Why? / Why not?)
- Tell us about a computer game you like.

The future

- What would you like to do for a living in the future? (Why?)
- If you could meet somebody famous, who would you choose?
- Are you going to go anywhere special soon? (Where?)
- How much longer will you continue studying English? (Why?)

Part 2 (4 minutes)

I'm going to give each of you two photographs. I'd like you to talk about your photographs on your own for about a minute, and also to answer a question about your partner's photographs.

(Candidate A), look at page 187 and photographs which show **people paying attention**. I'd like you to compare the photographs, and say **why it's important to pay attention in these situations**.

Thank you. *(Candidate B)*, **do you always pay attention when people talk to you?**

Now, *(Candidate B)*, turn to the photographs on page 188. They show **people meeting friends in different places**. I'd like you to compare the photographs, and say **why the friends may have chosen these places to meet**.

Thank you. *(Candidate A)*, **how often do you see your friends?**

Part 3 (4 minutes)

Now I'd like you to talk about something together for about two minutes. Now look at page 189.

I'd like you to imagine that a college wants to offer students a series of workshops called 'Skills for Life'. Here are some topics they are thinking about, and a question for you to discuss. First you have some time to look at the task.

Now talk to each other about **how useful the students might find each of these topics.**

Thank you. Now you have a minute to decide **which 'Skills for Life' workshops would be most popular with students.**

Part 4 (4 minutes)

Use the following questions in order, as appropriate:

*   **Do you think workshops like these are a good idea? (Why? / Why not?)**
*   **Do you think boys and girls need the same practical skills? (Why? / Why not?)**
*   **Do you find it difficult to ask other people for advice? (Why? / Why not?)**
*   **Do you think it's worth spending a lot of time trying to be the best at something? (Why? / Why not?)**
*   **Have you ever tried to teach somebody how to do something? How easy was it?**
*   **What other life skills do you think it's important for students to learn? (Why?)**

> *Select any of the following prompts, as appropriate:*
> *   **What do you think?**
> *   **Do you agree?**
> *   **And you?**

Thank you. That is the end of the test.

TEST 8

Part 1

For questions **1 – 8**, read the text below and decide which answer (**A**, **B**, **C** or **D**) best fits each gap. There is an example at the beginning (**0**).

In the exam, you mark your answers **on a separate answer sheet**.

Example:

0   **A** extremely   **B** greatly   **C** considerably   **D** highly

0	A	B	C	D
	▬	▭	▭	▭

Solar power

It's **(0)** .... hot in the Eldorado Valley in Nevada, USA. In midsummer, temperatures regularly **(1)** .... forty-five degrees centigrade. That's why farmers have no **(2)** .... but to wake up early. To get a day's work done before the heat becomes **(3)** .... , they have to be out in the fields soon after dawn. The heat also **(4)** .... why this is the perfect place to construct a solar-power plant.

Solar power works by using special mirrors that focus the **(5)** .... of the sun onto a chamber full of oil. This oil then **(6)** .... up to a temperature of almost four-hundred degrees centigrade. Steam from the hot oil is then used to generate electricity.

Solar power works best where the sun is constantly very hot, so deserts where very few people live are ideal. **(7)** .... with alternatives such as wind and wave energy, therefore, the installations themselves can have a less negative **(8)** .... on people's lives, on wildlife or on the environment.

1	**A** fetch	**B** arrive	**C** meet	**D** reach
2	**A** chance	**B** reason	**C** choice	**D** hope
3	**A** improper	**B** unbearable	**C** unsatisfactory	**D** impassable
4	**A** explains	**B** describes	**C** accounts	**D** persuades
5	**A** rays	**B** bars	**C** lights	**D** flashes
6	**A** burns	**B** goes	**C** heats	**D** rises
7	**A** judged	**B** compared	**C** opposed	**D** conflicted
8	**A** impact	**B** feedback	**C** outcome	**D** upshot

Part 2

For questions **9 – 16**, read the text below and think of the word which best fits each gap. Use only **one** word in each gap. There is an example at the beginning (**0**).

In the exam, you write your answers **IN CAPITAL LETTERS on a separate answer sheet**.

Example: | 0 | T | H | A | T | | | | | | | | | | | | | | | | |

Online shopping

There is no doubt **(0)** .... online shopping is both convenient and popular. A decade ago, everyone was predicting that traditional shopping centres would soon be a thing of the past. **(9)** .... all the advantages of online shopping, however, this hasn't happened. Having said that, the internet has changed the **(10)** .... people shop. Some consumers obviously enjoy their regular trip to the mall or supermarket, perhaps regarding it **(11)** .... a social occasion, whilst others are happy to give it a miss.

One thing does seem clear, however. The bigger the purchase the **(12)** .... likely we are to go online to gather information on the range of products **(13)** .... the market, and then compare prices, before we **(14)** .... to a decision. A new car is **(15)** .... of the biggest purchases people ever make, and buyers typically spend four to six weeks considering their choices. But very **(16)** .... people actually buy a car online. Perhaps it just feels too risky.

For questions **17 – 24**, read the text below. Use the word given in capitals at the end of some of the lines to form a word that fits in the gap **in the same line**. There is an example at the beginning (**0**).

In the exam, you write your answers **IN CAPITAL LETTERS on a separate answer sheet**.

Example: | **0** | F | A | S | T | E | S | T | | | | | | | | | | | |

The blind pilot

Miles Hilton-Barber wasn't the first person to fly a microlight aircraft
from London to Sydney, nor was he the (**0**) ....   **FAST**
The (**17**) .... thing about the flight is that Miles is blind. It was the   **AMAZE**
fulfilment of a dream for the adventurer, who has also climbed Mount
Kilimanjaro and run across the Gobi desert.

Miles flew with a sighted co-pilot, but relied on audio output from
his (**18**) .... instruments to find his way. 'It's a very simple form of   **NAVIGATE**
flying,' he says. 'But for a blind man it's (**19**) .... because you get   **WONDER**
to use a (**20**) .... of senses. Smells come up from the ground and   **VARY**
you feel the changes in wind and temperature.'

Miles flew through some very (**21**) .... weather, including a   **PLEASANT**
snowstorm and very bad turbulence. Although he was wearing a
seatbelt, it was still a very (**22**) .... experience. Miles' greatest   **FRIGHT**
(**23**) .... , however, is that the trip raised around two-million dollars   **ACHIEVE**
for the charity called Seeing is Believing which gives practical
(**24**) .... to blind people in developing countries.   **ASSIST**

For questions **25 – 30**, complete the second sentence so that it has a similar meaning to the first sentence, using the word given. **Do not change the word given**. You must use between **two** and **five** words, including the word given. Here is an example (**0**).

Example:

0   What type of music do you like best?

IS YOUR FAVOURITE

What .... type of music?

The gap can be filled with the words 'is your favourite', so you write:

Example: | **0** | *IS YOUR FAVOURITE*

In the exam, you write **only** the missing words **IN CAPITAL LETTERS on a separate answer sheet**.

---

25   If you want to join the website, you need to complete an online form.

FILL

It is .... online form, if you want to join the website.

26   Although he was wearing a waterproof coat, Jon's clothes still got wet.

EVEN

Jon's clothes didn't .... he was wearing a waterproof coat.

27   It's a shame I'm not able to play table tennis as well as my brother.

COULD

I .... table tennis as well as my brother.

28   If you don't pay by the deadline, you won't be allowed to go on the trip.

UNLESS

You won't be allowed to go on the trip .... deadline.

29   Teresa found the book about ballet dancers really fascinating.

BY

Teresa .... the book about ballet dancers.

30   As Rowena didn't buy her ticket in advance, she didn't get a discount.

HAD

If Rowena .... in advance, she would have got a discount.

You are going to read an extract from an article about a dancer. For questions **31 – 36**, choose the answer (**A**, **B, C** or **D**) which you think fits best according to the text.

In the exam, you mark your answers **on a separate answer sheet**.

Pauline Koner (1912–2001)

Pauline Koner was a highly influential dancer and dance teacher, especially known for her book Elements of Performance (1993), in which she carefully analyses the qualities that make dance performances remarkable. The personal aura of great performers is surely inimitable, but the principles upon which their art is built can be learnt. By teaching these, Pauline Koner was helping a new generation go its own way with flair and authority.

As a young child growing up in New York, Pauline Koner would dance whenever she heard music. After seeing a performance by the great ballerina Anna Pavlova, she set her heart on becoming a dancer. A family friend recommended that she studied under Michel Fokine, the famous local ballet teacher. But Pauline's parents were dismayed to find he charged $5 a lesson, an unheard-of sum in the 1920s. Pauline's father, a well-known lawyer, came to an agreement with Fokine: he would offer his legal services in exchange for the ballet lessons. Pauline loved Fokine, but classical ballet was not quite for her. 'I couldn't express what I wanted in toe shoes,' she recalled. 'My feet hurt too much.'

Pauline went on to study Spanish dance and several types of Asian dance, and she performed with dancers who combined Asian dance with their own particular modern movements. In 1930, Pauline was offered her first solo concert. The originality of this delighted John Martin, an influential critic on The New York Times, and he declared that the programme 'exhibited her unquestionable fight to stand alone.' Pauline continued to dance solos around the world, touring Egypt and Palestine in 1932. She also taught and performed in the Soviet Union from 1934 to 1936, one of the first American dancers to appear there.

Pauline Koner was always curious about the customs, costumes and dances of other nations. As a child, she would paste National Geographic photos into scrapbooks. She thought that she was able to 'absorb' divergent styles and influences because, as she put it: 'Dance was so much my life that when I studied a dance form, I was really living that way of dancing and not just keeping in shape.' She was convinced that students could also 'absorb' other dance forms provided that 'they don't allow themselves to be overwhelmed by a single technique.'

Although usually considered a modern dancer, Pauline enjoyed pointing out that she had never had a modern dance lesson in her life. Rather, she developed her own modern style after studying a remarkable variety of other styles. But why did she never study modern dance? Pauline answered that question with a bit of history. In the late 1920s, modern dance was so new that there were few modern dance schools in America. By 1930 there were some, but Pauline had already established herself as an artist: she had, in effect, become a modern dancer entirely on her own.

Then in 1945 came a momentous change in Pauline's artistic life. After one of her programmes, a modern dance choreographer called Doris Humphrey, whom she particularly admired, sent Pauline a note filled with praise. Yet it **30** also contained some criticism. Pauline found this so perceptive that she asked Humphrey to be her choreographic adviser, her 'outside eye', as she liked to call it. Doris Humphrey served as artistic adviser to the Limón Dance **32** Company in the 1940s and 1950s, and they found Pauline such a kindred spirit that they invited her to be what they called a 'permanent guest artist' with them. The rest, as they say, is history.

31 As a child, how did Pauline feel about Michel Fokine's lessons?

A She worried that her parents couldn't really afford them.

B She felt they didn't really bring out her real talent.

C She feared they would damage her physically.

D She saw them as her only chance to learn.

32 What do we learn about Pauline in the third paragraph?

A She challenged the political leaders of her time.

B She was better known abroad than in her own country.

C She received some praise for her attempt to be different.

D She was finding it difficult to create a style that suited her.

33 What did Pauline say about 'absorbing' different styles of dance?

A It was something that came naturally to her.

B She felt she was unfairly criticised for doing it.

C She accepted that she had a unique talent for it.

D It started out as a way of improving her fitness levels.

34 When modern dance schools became more common, Pauline felt that

A their standards were low.

B she didn't have need of one.

C she'd like to start one herself.

D there were still not enough of them.

35 What does the word 'this' in line **30** refer to?

A some criticism

B a modern dance

C Pauline's 'outside eye'

D praise for Pauline's work

36 The expression 'kindred spirit' in line **32** is used to emphasise Pauline's

A boundless enthusiasm.

B successful initiatives.

C outgoing personality.

D general approach.

Part 6

You are going to read an article about converting a boat into a home. Six sentences have been removed from the article. Choose from the sentences **A – G** the one which fits each gap (**37 – 42**). There is one extra sentence you do not need to use.

In the exam, you mark your answers **on a separate answer sheet**.

Making a boat into a home

When Vib Mason moved to London from the countryside a few years ago, she wanted to buy a flat. 'It was very depressing – I couldn't afford a decent place,' she says. So she started to consider other options. She'd once lived on a small wooden yacht with her ex-husband, so she put the word about amongst boating friends to look out for any good deals. Six weeks later, she'd found two boats for sale: a barge and a 30 x 7 metre tugboat, a small but powerful boat used for guiding large ships into harbours.

Vib and her new partner, Adrian, immediately fell for the tugboat. 'The barge was in much better condition, and it would have been an easy job,' says Vib. **37** A month later, it was theirs. 'Friends took one look and told us we were crazy,' she says. 'We had nowhere to keep it and a 27-tonne engine was taking up 80 square metres of valuable living space!'

The small interior was divided into tiny rooms and there were no windows below deck **38** This included a small kitchen that had been used by seamen for fifty years. And the steel body of the boat was in perfect condition. 'We didn't even check for holes when we bought it,' Vib says.

Finding a permanent home for the boat wasn't easy – none of the marinas Vib visited was helpful. 'One owner said he didn't have a space for the tugboat, but I noticed room at the back of the marina on the outside. **39** he said. The boat fitted like a glove.'

Then the hard work started. Vib suggested Adrian might like to do the work needed on the boat and she'd finance it. **40** The timing was right, too, as Adrian had grown tired of his job in the city. 'It was no good, I spent too much time sitting behind a desk. I nearly died when I started work on the boat because I was so unfit.'

They now have a kitchen-diner, a small sitting room, a bathroom, a utility room, three cabins and a small office. The former engine room is a huge living area. The worst job was cleaning the bilges, the small gap between the floorboards and the bottom of the boat, which were coated in thick oil. **41** Eventually, they paid a specialist £2,000 to do it.

Living on the boat has its quirks. It can get uncomfortable if the boat moves too much. **42** says Vib. The tide produces different sensations on the boat, depending on whether it's floating or resting on the mud. 'When it's hot in summer, it's great when the tide's in and you're floating, but when it's blowing a gale, I prefer to be on the mud. But we love it, he adds, and we love the shape of the boat and the fact that even now it's retained some of its original character.'

A	He'd worked with wood, done a bit of building and made surfboards.	**E**	If you can get the boat in there, you can have it.
B	But you could live on different levels on the tugboat.	**F**	This was such a daunting task that they ignored it for two years.
C	Because it's at the end of the marina, it feels as if it's in the middle of the sea.	**G**	However, upstairs all the original accommodation was intact.
D	Some old floorboards from a friend's cottage became the flooring in the bedroom.		

Part 7

You are going to read a magazine article about four young fashion designers. For questions **43 – 52**, choose from the designers (**A – D**). The designers may be chosen more than once.

In the exam, you mark your answers **on a separate answer sheet**.

Which designer ...

appreciates the fact that the course wasn't as specialised as some?	**43**
feels that the college benefits from its significance in local society?	**44**
got ideas for designs from an outdoor activity?	**45**
feels more creative as a result of choosing this college?	**46**
likes the idea of mixing with rich and famous people?	**47**
wanted to reflect the history of the college in certain designs?	**48**
decided to study in a city that had fewer distractions for a student?	**49**
chose to make clothes from hard-wearing materials?	**50**
was pleased to learn skills not directly related to fashion?	**51**
found inspiration in a family connection with fashion?	**52**

New kids on the frock

Edinburgh is a great place to study fashion, according to four recent graduates

A   Stewart Parvin

I chose to study in Edinburgh because I thought there would be fewer social temptations there than in London, and I wanted to concentrate on my work. It was a great place to be a student because we felt like we were at the heart of everything – an important part of the city – you don't get that everywhere. My approach has always been very commercial, and I was lucky in that I was encouraged to explore that, even though others on the course were more creative and original. A lot of colleges are either one thing or the other – creative or commercial – but we had a good mix. The college was also included in Graduate Fashion Week in London. It's a high-profile event and so some very talented students were attracted to the course as a result. Studying with them hasn't done me any harm at all.

B   Zoe Donald

I was keen to make my graduate collection very personal. I graduated in the college's centenary year, and I thought about how much paper it must have got through over that time, and made my designs to reflect that idea. My granny was a very glamorous model and a few years ago I inherited her wardrobe, which also gave me ideas. I've really enjoyed my course. The great thing about it is that it feels like part of an art college, rather than just a fashion course. There's a lot of interaction with the rest of the departments, and so I've done a bit of graphics and sculpture, too. But I don't think my own particular ideas fit in very well in Edinburgh generally, so I may not stay. I'd love the opportunity to work with a top London designer, but we'll have to wait and see.

C   David Fraser

A main focus of my collection is a big prominent knot somewhere in each outfit, on a sleeve or on a shoulder, and I've looked to knots in sailing for inspiration. I also get ideas from a designer called Halston – his minimalist designs and the simple elegance of his cutting. I'm also attracted to the fact. that he was the first celebrity designer, and I have to admit that side of the industry does appeal to me. I love London, so I'm looking forward to going down there. You really have to make your own opportunities in Scotland, and it's tough establishing yourself as a young designer. I don't know what the future holds, but I like the idea of working in an established fashion house, and my dream is to be a creative director of a leading house somewhere.

D   Rachel Barrett

I like to design clothes that I'd wear myself. I began the work for my graduate collection by looking at shapes in traditional Mongolian dress. I wanted to use durable fabrics, so my collection includes a lot of leather, which makes it look a bit punky, but it's not really a retro style. I wanted to study fashion although my parents are both architects, so I guess they allowed me to indulge my artistic side. The great thing about ECA is that the studio is a really great environment in which to work. Studying here instead of London has meant that I'm free from all the influences there, so I've developed my own style, though we all have to go to London to source the fabrics for our collections because they're just not available here. Although I'd like to set up my own label at some point, initially I'm looking for employment.

Part I

You **must** answer this question. Write your answer in **140 – 190** words in an appropriate style.

1   In your English class you have been discussing ways that students can find out about different types of work. Now your English teacher has asked you to write an essay.

Write an essay using **all** the notes and giving reasons for your point of view.

How can students learn something about different types of work?

Notes

Write about:

1. taking part in voluntary work

2. watching videos about jobs online

3. .... (your own idea)

Write your **essay**.

Write an answer to **one** of the questions **2 – 4** in this part. Write your answer in **140 – 190** words in an appropriate style.

2   You have seen this announcement in an international magazine.

> # Customs and traditions of my country
>
> Tell us about the customs and traditions in your country, and say where tourists might be able to go to see them.
>
> We will publish the most interesting articles in next month's issue.

Write your **article**.

3   You have received this email from your English-speaking friend, Sally, who is giving a presentation about your country. Write an email to Sally, giving her the information she needs.

> I'd like to tell them about the music young people listen to – or do we all listen to the same bands?
>
> Also, how much of their free time teenagers spend at home, and where they go to have fun.
>
> Write soon!
>
> Sally

Write your **email**.

4   A well-known sports celebrity recently visited your college to talk to students about his/her life and career. Now the college principal has asked you to write a report saying:

- what main topics were discussed
- how useful the visit was for the students
- whether future visits by other celebrities are a good idea and why

Write your **report**.

Part I

You will hear people talking in eight different situations. For questions **1 – 8**, choose the best answer (**A**, **B** or **C**).

1   You hear part of an interview with the conductor of an orchestra.
    What does he say about physical fitness?
    A   He's learnt the value of regular exercise.
    B   It's unusual for conductors to get an injury.
    C   Older conductors need to pay more attention to it.

2   You hear part of an interview with an interior designer.
    What does she recommend about picture frames?
    A   Don't waste too much money on specialised glass.
    B   See the frame as part of the cost of your picture.
    C   Try to buy a picture that already has one.

3   You hear part of a programme about a new gadget.
    What does the gadget do?
    A   It tells you how healthy food made at home really is.
    B   It allows you to cook food outside of the home.
    C   It keeps homemade food warm.

4   You overhear two people talking about a film they've seen.
    What did the man dislike about it?
    A   the pace was too slow
    B   the acting was not good
    C   the plot was hard to follow

5   You hear part of a soap opera about life in a school.
    Which character is talking?
    A   a sports teacher
    B   the headteacher
    C   a parent

6   You hear a girl talking about a rucksack she's just bought.
    Who does she like about it?
    A   It's light.
    B   It's large.
    C   It's waterproof.

7   You hear some information about a competition.
    People entering the competition answer a question about
    A   literature.
    B   cinema.
    C   music.

8   You hear part of a programme about a holiday destination.
    The presenter is making the point that
    A   mass tourism is spoiling it.
    B   it needs to offer better facilities.
    C   the local inhabitants are leaving.

You will hear an announcement about a competition for young composers. For questions **9 – 18**, complete the sentences with a word or short phrase.

Competition for young composers

Young composers interested in taking part must send in both their

(9) .... and a recording.

Participants will then attend what's called **(10)** ....
led by well-known composers.

On the day, participants must bring their most recent piece of work as well as their

(11) ....

All participants will get help from **(12)** ....
musicians on the day.

In last year's competition, most participants chose music for the

(13) .... as their favourite style.

Participants must submit pieces which are no longer than

(14) .... minutes.

The judges will be looking for **(15)** ....
as the most important quality of compositions.

For best results, participants are advised not to compose music on a

(16) ....

Schools and colleges will be informed about the winners by

(17) .... if not before.

As one of the prizes, winning compositions will be performed at the

(18) ....

Part 3

You will hear five short extracts in which people are talking about travel websites. For questions **19 – 23**, choose from the list (**A – H**) what each speaker says about the website they used. There are three extra letters which you do not need to use.

A   It has clear information and is easy to navigate

B   I received prompt replies to my email enquiries.

C   I got my money back when I cancelled a booking.

D   It's better for some destinations than others.

E   I was offered the lowest prices on the market.

F   I wasn't allowed to change my travel plans.

G   It failed to deliver some services it promised.

H   I found the feedback from other users useful.

Speaker 1		19
Speaker 2		20
Speaker 3		21
Speaker 4		22
Speaker 5		23

You will hear an interview with a professional photographer called Jane Thorpe. For questions **24 – 30**, choose the best answer (**A, B** or **C**).

24   What reason does Jane give for not doing a college photography course?

   A   She couldn't afford the fees.
   B   She feared it might waste her time.
   C   She was following her father's advice.

25   What does Jane say about the places where she takes her photos?

   A   She doesn't choose them herself.
   B   She does a lot of research into them.
   C   She finds them all equally interesting.

26   Jane says that up to the year 2004, she

   A   found it difficult to make a living.
   B   lacked a feeling of achievement.
   C   spent too long on single projects.

27   What gives Jane most pleasure during a photography trip?

   A   encounters with a variety of people
   B   a feeling of freedom she experiences
   C   the thought that others will see her photos

28   What does Jane like least about her work?

   A   having to do lots of office work
   B   being unable to pursue a hobby
   C   having hardly any social life

29   Jane believes that a professional photographer should

   A   concentrate on just one area of photography.
   B   hire someone to do the business management .
   C   get feedback from other professionals.

30   What advice does Jane give amateur photographers?

   A   get plenty of practice
   B   Invest in the best available equipment
   C   read technical books on the subject

Part 1 (2 minutes)

The examiner will ask you a few questions about yourself and what you think about different things. For example, the examiner might ask you about:

Everyday life

* Do you go to bed late at weekends? (Why? / Why not?)
* How often do you have meals with your family at home? (Why? / Why not?)
* What's your favourite leisure activity at weekends? (Tell us about it)
* How often do you chat with your friends when you're at home? (Why?)

Fitness and health

* Which sports do you enjoy doing or watching? (Why?)
* Is it important to eat food which is good for your health? (Why? / Why not?)
* Some people say that sitting for a long time is bad for you. What's your opinion?
* Is there a new free-time activity you'd take up if you had more time? (Tell us about it.)

Education and work

* Do you think the subjects you studied at school will be useful for your future? (Why? / Why not?)
* If you had time to learn a new language, which one would you choose? (Why?)
* Which was your favourite subject at school? (Why?)
* Do you work / study better in the morning or the evening? (Why?)

Part 2 (4 minutes)

I'm going to give each of you two photographs. I'd like you to talk about your photographs on your own for about a minute, and also to answer a question about your partner's photographs.

(Candidate A), look at page 190 and photographs which show **people getting ready for something**. I'd like you to compare the photographs, and say **how the people might be feeling**.

Thank you. *(Candidate B)*, **do you take a long time to get ready in the morning?**

Now, *(Candidate B)*, turn to the photographs on page 191. They show **people listening**. I'd like you to compare the photographs, and say **how important it is for the people to listen carefully**.

Thank you. *(Candidate A)*, **do you listen to music when you're studying?**

Part 3 (4 minutes)

Now I'd like you to talk about something together for about two minutes. Now look at page 192.

Here are some aspects of social media which people think are important, and a question for you to discuss. First you have some time to look at the task.

Now talk to each other about **why people think these aspects of social media are important**.

Thank you. Now you have a minute to decide **which two aspects are the least important**.

Part 4 (4 minutes)

Use the following questions in order, as appropriate:

- **Some people say you can't protect your privacy on social media. What's your opinion?**
- **Do you think people should check messages on their phones, wherever they are? (Why? / Why not?)**
- **At what age should children be allowed to have their own phone? (Why?)**
- **What's the best way to communicate with friends you don't see very often? (Why?)**
- **Is it important to have the most up-to-date phone? (Why? / Why not?)**
- **Some people like the idea of spending time on a desert island without any means of communication. What do you think?**

Select any of the following prompts, as appropriate:

- **What do you think?**
- **Do you agree?**
- **And you?**

Thank you. That is the end of the test.

SPEAKING BANK

Part I

In this part of the test, you will answer a few questions on personal topics such as your home, your daily routine, your work, likes and dislikes, etc.

Watch the full test online.

Exam help

✓ You know the answer to these questions, so reply confidently and add interesting information.

✓ Avoid making basic grammar mistakes. Think about the verb tense you are going to use: is the question about the past, the present or the future?

✓ Activate the vocabulary area of the question. For example, if the question is about your favourite type of TV programme, think of comedies, soap operas, news, quizzes, etc.

✓ Speak clearly so that your partner and the two examiners can understand everything you say.

Useful language

Communicative strategies

Sorry, can you say that again?
Sorry, I didn't quite catch that.
Would you mind repeating that, please?
Do you mean … ?
Well, that's an interesting question.
Now, how can I put this?

Giving personal information

I have two siblings and we all get on very well. That's why …
My house is rather small, just … , but I love it because …
Although I have lots of friends/family, I don't see them very often because …
To be honest, I'm not very good at …

Responding to questions about everyday life and interests

I'm studying … now, but I'd really like to … in the future.
I used to be very keen on … but now …
I don't like … , really, though I do enjoy …
My favourite time to … is … because …
I'm not very sure what I'll do, but I may decide to …

In this part of the test, you will speak on your own for one minute. You will compare two photographs and say something else about them.

Watch the full test online.

Exam help

- ✔ Remember that you have not been asked to describe the photos but to compare them. There is no time to comment in detail on one photo at a time. Start off by comparing the people, the places and the situations and give a personal reaction to the pictures.
- ✔ Use the question written above the photographs to remind yourself that after you have compared the photos, you have to do the second task. In the second part, you are asked to speculate, i.e. to say what you think and give opinions.
- ✔ Use varied vocabulary and try to use comparative forms correctly.
- ✔ Don't stop to search for a word you don't remember. Explain what you want to say in other words.

Useful language

Comparing

The people in the photos are in very different places.
In the first photo they are … , whereas in the second photo …
These are very different activities …
The type of food these children are preparing is very different …
I can see some similarities in these photos, they have the same …
This first photo is more/less attractive than the second because …
These girls seem to be having a better time than the girls in …
The situations are very different, here people are enjoying … whilst here they are …

Speculating

Perhaps they have decided to do this because …
The people seem to be enjoying …
I get the impression that the woman …
The girl looks like she is feeling …
He may have chosen to stay at home because …
I think this man looks really tired; he may have been working all day.
The family in the first photo are probably at home.
I think these people may be feeling rather nervous because …

In this part of the test, you will discuss a task with your partner. You will both initiate discussion of the different written prompts in turn, and respond to each other's comments.

Watch the full test online.

Exam help

✓ Focus on the first task you are given, which requires you to discuss the options for two minutes. To remind yourself of the task, look back at the question printed in the central box.

✓ Remember that after the two-minute discussion, you will be given a one-minute decision-making task. Don't come to a decision too soon because you may then struggle to find other things to say.

✓ When your partner gives an opinion on a written prompt, respond fully before moving to something else. It does not matter if you do not discuss all the prompts, what is important is that you produce sufficient language at the right level.

✓ If your partner seems happy to let you do the talking, do involve him/her by asking his/her opinions. You will be given credit for doing that.

Useful language

Inviting your partner's opinion and taking turns

I think concentration is essential when you want to win.

It depends on whether the film has a complex plot or not.

There's no point in studying unless you can concentrate. What do you think?

Frankly, I don't think this an activity which requires much concentration.

Following up on your partner's opinions

I'm sure that's what it is, I agree.

As I see it, …

In my opinion, …

That's an interesting point, but I think …

As you said, this job must be really challenging. However, …

I take your point, but …

I'm afraid I don't agree. I think …

Well, I would say that …

Moving to another written prompt

Right, why don't we talk about … ?

How about this idea? Do you want to say something about it?

Now, moving on, …

Shall we discuss this idea next?

I'm not sure what this means. What do you think?

Part 4

In this part of the test, you will take part in a discussion by answering questions which broaden the topic of Part 3. You can also respond to what your partner says.

Watch the full test online.

Exam help

✔ Remember that these questions require more extended responses than those in Part 1. Don't be afraid to talk about your opinions and feelings. The examiner only wants you to produce some complex language to show off your level.

✔ There is no 'correct' answer to the questions and you will not be assessed on what you think, but you should always give reasons and back up your opinions.

✔ You are encouraged to contribute ideas to what your partner says, even if the question was not addressed to you.

✔ You have now warmed up and this is the last part of your test. Enjoy the interaction and the feeling that you can express your ideas with confidence!

Useful language

Giving opinions

Well, personally, I feel …
People often say that … , but I …
People often complain that … , and I agree.
I don't think that is the answer to …
I'd do something different …
I think it is unlikely that anybody would …
Yes, I think young people have much more freedom than …
No, that's not the way I see things.
I'm not sure, to be honest.
My friends/family/teachers think I am wrong, but I believe …

Giving examples and/or reasons

I can think of a few examples of this, …
For example, when you …
I once had an experience which …
To clarify what I mean, I can give you …
There are many reasons for this …
People dislike … . This is because …
People often don't tell the truth. That's why I …
Just think of all the problems that causes. To begin with …

WRITING BANK

Test 1, Task 1

You **must** answer this question. Write your answer in **140 – 190** words in an appropriate style.

In your English class you have been discussing the use of communication technology such as phones and tablets in our everyday lives. Now your English teacher has asked you to write an essay.

Write an essay using **all** the notes and giving reasons for your point of view.

Sample answer

Can we live happily without using communication technology all the time?

Most people agree that it would be impossible to live happily without our phones or tablets. They are an essential part of our lives.

We need them mostly for instant communication with family and friends, a truly vital link. It is not only that: phones have our music on them, take photos and video and enable us to watch films or TV.

However, it is worrying when people cannot enjoy an experience because they are constantly involved with their phones. It feels impolite and wrong when people in a meeting, or in a restaurant having a meal with friends, pay more attention to their phones than to the people they are with.

I believe we can learn to be less dependent. First, we can decide to check our messages less often, accepting that we do not have to be constantly available and we do not have to respond immediately. Second, we can turn off our devices when we are not alone, to give the people we are with our full attention.

To sum up, we cannot live happily without our phones. But we can learn to use them sensibly.

You can introduce the subject by rephrasing the sentence you will discuss.

Use one topic for each paragraph.

Using words such as 'first' and 'second' may help you to organise the ideas in your essay.

Your conclusion should be a summary of the ideas you have expressed earlier.

Useful language

Introduction

I think this topic is really important.
Most people agree that …
People often disagree about …
You often hear people say that …

Linking ideas

It is true that … However, we should …
This is a good explanation, but that is not all.
It is not just that our social life would suffer, it is also …

Giving opinions

I believe we can learn to be …
It is worrying when people …
It seems to me that …
I am convinced that this is the right thing to do.

Conclusion

To sum up, whilst it is true that …
Taking all of this into account, I believe …
Having presented all the arguments, it seems clear to me that …
Finally, I feel very strongly that …

Exam help

- ✓ Read the essay question carefully and plan what you want to include in four or five paragraphs. See a sample essay plan on 163.
- ✓ Jot down ideas for each paragraph and possible language. You need topic-related vocabulary and some complex sentences using linking words.
- ✓ You are presenting your point of view and need to support it with reasons or evidence.
- ✓ Make sure you use a formal or semi-formal style. Avoid using informal language.

Planning your essay

Aim to write five paragraphs.

Paragraph 1

The introduction. Try to write two sentences to avoid a single-sentence paragraph. The first sentence can be a re-phrasing of the essay title. The second sentence can be a very brief outline of some of the ideas you are going to include.

Paragraph 2

Deal with the first note: phones or other devices we can't live without.

Paragraph 3

Deal with the second note: to use or not to use phones in certain social situations.

Paragraph 4

Deal with the third note (your own): how to reduce our dependence

Paragraph 5

The conclusion. Summarise your main opinions by referring briefly to the points mentioned in paragraphs 2, 3 and 4. Try to write at least two sentences to avoid a single-sentence paragraph.

How to use the written notes

Each note will be just a few words long. The note on its own will not give you sufficient material. Before you start writing, take a few minutes to expand them. Here's a way to do it:

1   Write down the notes (including your own) and draw three lines from each one. Now concentrate on each note in turn. Try to think of three ideas that can add content to that note. For example:

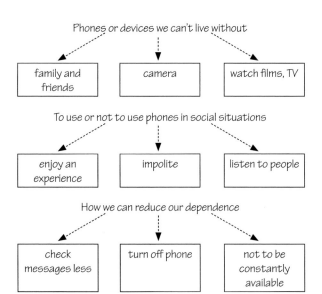

Phones or devices we can't live without

| family and friends | camera | watch films, TV |

To use or not to use phones in social situations

| enjoy an experience | impolite | listen to people |

How we can reduce our dependence

| check messages less | turn off phone | not to be constantly available |

2   Choose the best ideas from your notes and start writing.

Checklist

Checklist

When you finish writing an essay, use this checklist:

Content
Have you covered the two notes given and one of your own?

Communicative achievement
Is your style correct for an essay, i.e. is it fairly formal? Are your opinions easy to follow?

Organisation
Have you divided your writing into paragraphs, with an introduction and a conclusion?

Language
Have you used:
• some complex sentences using linking words?
• a variety of grammatical structures and tenses?
• some interesting vocabulary?

Part 2 Report

Test 1, Task 4

Write an answer to one of the questions **2 – 4** in this part. Write your answer in **140 – 190** words in an appropriate style.

A new sports centre opened recently in your area and a community website has asked you to write a report, giving your opinions about the following:

- how good the facilities for the more popular sports are.
- how welcoming the reception staff and sports trainers are.
- what the prices for students and other people are like.

Write your **report**.

Sample answer

In the first paragraph say what the purpose of your report is.

The use of headings allows you to organise the sections of your report clearly.

Try to include some complex sentences by using linking words.

Include a final sentence or two summarising your conclusions.

Report on the new sports centre

This is a report about the new sports centre, a much-needed facility for this area, which has finally opened.

The sports available

There is an impressive hall for a range of popular sports, such as basketball, netball, volleyball and badminton. The fitness studio is spacious, with exercise equipment that includes weights as well as running machines. And the star attraction is the 25-metre swimming pool, with a sauna and excellent changing rooms.

The staff

The reception staff are very helpful and ready to give customers all the information they may need. The centre offers a number of activities and courses for all ages, from swimming lessons to exercise classes to karate lessons, all taught by specialist trainers who seem very keen to give everyone a chance to improve their skills.

Prices

Prices range from one-year memberships at £300 to monthly passes that cost £30. I was surprised to find out that they are not offering special prices for students, but was told by the manager that there are plans to introduce discounts soon. My conclusion is this is definitely an excellent sports centre which offers just what our community needs.

Useful language

Introducing the report

This is a report about …
The aim of this report is …
In this report I will …
I have been asked to write a report about …

Giving opinions

There is an impressive range of …
This is definitely an excellent …
I was surprised to find out that …
The star attraction here is no doubt …

Finishing the report

My conclusion is that …
To conclude, I would say that …
In conclusion, I think that …
The main conclusion of my report is …
Taking everything into account, I conclude that …

Exam help

- ✔ Read the question carefully and plan your report before you start to write. Think of the format you are going to use and whether you are going to use headings.
- ✔ Remember you have to write approximately 180 words, so don't write too much under any one heading.
- ✔ Remember you have to show a range of language, so use interesting vocabulary and write full sentences, linking some of your ideas to produce some complex sentences.
- ✔ Include a conclusion, even if it is short.
- ✔ Check that you have used a semi-formal or formal style and correct any informal language you may have used.

Part 2 Article

Test 1, Task 2

Useful language

Introducing an article about a person

I will always remember …

I've never met anybody like …

X is the most amazing person I've ever come across.

When I met X, I just knew he/she was incredibly special.

Rhetorical questions

Is Susie still in my heart? She definitely is.

How would you react in a situation like this?

Was I surprised? Well, no, not really.

Did you have an unforgettable childhood friend?

Describing people and past events

I admired her because she was …

She was an only child, while I …

We would spend long hours …

We were always the ones who …

Exam help

✔ Read the question carefully and plan your article before you start to write. Pay attention to who you are writing the article for. If it is for your school magazine, you may use an informal style. If it is for a magazine with a wider readership, you may need a semi-formal style.

✔ Write down some interesting, colourful language that you may want to use. Remember that the purpose of your article is not only to inform but also to entertain the reader.

✔ Think of an interesting title.

✔ Use interesting details, examples or anecdotes to ensure that your article has a personal touch.

Write an answer to one of the questions **2 – 4** in this part. Write your answer in **140 – 190** words in an appropriate style.

You have seen an announcement in an international magazine.

MY CHILDHOOD FRIEND

Tell us about your best friend when you were a child and say why you got on well together.

The best article will win a book.

Write your **article**.

Sample answer

My childhood friend

I will always remember Susie, my wonderful childhood friend. I was eight years old and she was eight and a half. Susie was an only child who always had her parents' undivided attention, while I had three younger siblings. I admired her because she was impulsive, outgoing and great fun, and she always seemed completely self-confident. I think she liked me because I was cautious and sensible and she could trust me. But the most important reason we got on so well was that we shared a passion for making up stories.

We both wanted to be writers when we grew up. Susie was the main author of the incredible plots we wrote together. The stories were full of nasty characters: Susie and me were always the heroines who taught them a lesson. We would spend long hours thinking up possible endings for our stories. The best thing about it was that nobody else knew what we were up to. It was our secret life.

Our friendship ended when we were twelve because we moved to different schools and lost touch. Is Susie still in my heart? She definitely is.

Introduce your article with a catchy sentence to attract attention.

These two sentences are a good summary of why you liked each other

A good interesting closing sentence for this paragraph engages the reader.

This is good way of combining a few bits of information to produce a complex sentence.

Part 2 Letter

Test 1, Task 3

You have seen this advertisement for a part-time job and you want to apply.

Write an answer to one of the questions **2 – 4** in this part. Write your answer in **140 – 190** words in an appropriate style.

World Tours Agency

We need a young person to show a group of English-speaking teenagers round this area.

Are you the energetic and sociable person we're looking for?

Are you available in August?

Are you fluent in English?

Do you get on well with teenagers?

Write to **Sam Bastion, the manager**.

Write your **letter**.

Sample answer

Use a formal opening, with a comma at the end.

Always start by stating what the purpose of your letter is.

Organise your content points into paragraphs: this one deals with the third point in the task: your fluency in English.

This is a good way to end a formal letter.

Dear Mr Bastion,

I am writing because I am interested in the part-time job you advertised. I am available for the whole of August, including weekends.

I have lots of energy and enthusiasm and can work for hours with only short breaks. I am also a sociable person who loves contact with people from all over the world. I'm known for being open and easy to communicate with. My friends say I am good at explaining things and at talking about a range of subjects.

I'm good at English and was able to use it when we welcomed Canadian students to our college. I was their interpreter. I also have a certificate from the University of Cambridge which states that my spoken level of English is enough for everyday situations.

I get on well with people of all ages, but particularly well with teenagers. As I have two teenage sisters, I have lots of contact with them and their friends. I'm twenty years old and I think I know exactly what teenagers would expect to get from a visit to this area.

I look forward to hearing from you.

Yours sincerely,

Martin Bruno

Useful language

Talking about yourself

I am a sociable person who loves contact with …

I am very reliable and get on well with people …

I have always had an interest in …

I think I am the right person for this job because …

Talking about your experience

I was able to use my English when …

I have helped to organise a number of college events.

I've always enjoyed working with young people.

I have some experience of working as a group leader.

Talking about your availability

I am available for the whole of August, including weekends.

I would be able to start immediately.

At the moment I am only available … but I would be able to work … next month.

Exam help

✓ Read the question carefully to decide the level of formality. The task does not tell you that you have to write a formal letter, you can decide.

✓ Underline the points in the question. Decide how many paragraphs you want to write and which points you will include in each one.

✓ Note down the ideas you want to use for each point. Don't start writing until you have some ideas.

✓ When you write about your experience, give clear details and examples. Be imaginative and remember you don't have to be truthful!

Part 3 Email

Test 2, Task 2

Useful language

Informal openings

Dear Simon, Hello Simon,
Hi Simon, Simon.

Suggesting activities

There are several museums which might interest you.
Here's what I suggest.
I think you'll love the …
If you're interested, we could visit …

Reassuring remarks

Don't worry, I've been looking at activities …
Leave it to me, I'll buy the tickets.
There's no need for you to worry about anything.
I'll make sure that everything is ready for you.

Informal closings

See you soon!
All the best
Love

Exam help

✓ Read the instructions and the email from your friend very carefully, noting down all the information you need to include.

✓ Decide what to include in each paragraph and jot down some vocabulary you may want to use.

✓ Try to write close to the maximum number of words.

Write an answer to **one** of the questions **2 – 4** in this part. Write your answer in **140 – 190** words in an appropriate style.

Your English friend is coming to visit you next month and this is part of an email he has sent you.

I'm looking forward to this trip, but you know me, I like to plan everything! I'd like to go and see as much music as possible, without spending too much, and also visit some museums. Have you had any thoughts about how we could make the most of the week?

Simon

Write your **email**.

Sample answer

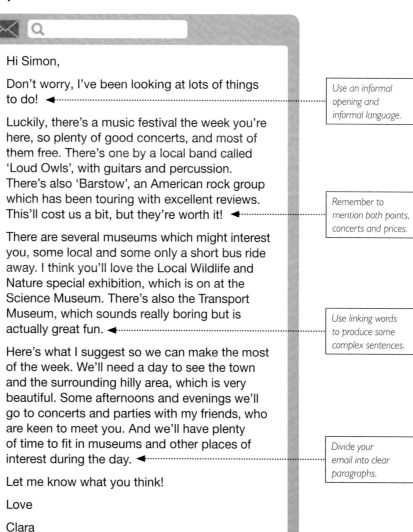

Hi Simon,

Don't worry, I've been looking at lots of things to do! ◄· · · · · · · · · · · · · · · · · · ·

Use an informal opening and informal language.

Luckily, there's a music festival the week you're here, so plenty of good concerts, and most of them free. There's one by a local band called 'Loud Owls', with guitars and percussion. There's also 'Barstow', an American rock group which has been touring with excellent reviews. This'll cost us a bit, but they're worth it! ◄· · · · · ·

Remember to mention both points, concerts and prices.

There are several museums which might interest you, some local and some only a short bus ride away. I think you'll love the Local Wildlife and Nature special exhibition, which is on at the Science Museum. There's also the Transport Museum, which sounds really boring but is actually great fun. ◄· · · · · ·

Use linking words to produce some complex sentences.

Here's what I suggest so we can make the most of the week. We'll need a day to see the town and the surrounding hilly area, which is very beautiful. Some afternoons and evenings we'll go to concerts and parties with my friends, who are keen to meet you. And we'll have plenty of time to fit in museums and other places of interest during the day. ◄· · · · · ·

Divide your email into clear paragraphs.

Let me know what you think!

Love

Clara

Part 2 Review

Test 2, Task 3

Write an answer to **one** of the questions **2 – 4** in this part. Write your answer in **140 – 190** words in an appropriate style.

You recently saw this notice in the local newspaper.

Write a review of a TV nature programme and win a camera!

Include information about the content of the programme and the locations where it was filmed, and say whether you think people of all ages would enjoy it.

Write your **review**.

Sample answer

Start by introducing the subject and giving a summary of your opinions about the programme.

In this paragraph, describe the content of the programme, which may include details about the animals, the way it was filmed, the purpose of the programme. You can deal with the locations in the second paragraph.

Don't be afraid of expressing your personal feelings.

Use interesting descriptive language to give the reader a clear idea of what you saw.

'Giraffes, Africa's Gentle Giants' is without a doubt one of the most interesting and instructive TV nature programmes I have ever seen.

It is about the incredible efforts of one scientist and his international team to protect endangered African giraffes by finding them a new home and transporting them there – a truly daring plan. You hear that giraffe numbers have dropped by almost twenty per cent because they are threatened by wild fires and illegal hunters. You watch these wonderful animals, filmed by day and at night and it is a fascinating, moving spectacle.

The locations vary from the stunning African savanna, which is rolling grassland with some trees, to the mighty river Nile. The giraffes' new home is on the other side of the river Nile, so you first watch the team's extraordinary job of catching twenty giraffes securely, then you see them taking the giraffes on a huge boat across the river, to a wilder, safer area.

I believe everyone who loves nature and wants to protect it would enjoy this programme, whatever their age. They would also learn a lot from it, as I did.

Useful language

Introducing the programme

This programme is about …
This programme takes the viewer into the world of …
If you are looking for suspense, this is the programme to watch.

Giving positive and negative opinions

This is the best nature programme I have ever seen.
Viewers may find some of the commentaries difficult to follow.
Some scenes are breathtaking.
I wish it had shown more detail …

Recommending

I would recommend it to anyone who loves adventure.
This is an excellent … for teenagers, but I don't think it would appeal to …
This is excellent for all ages, though children may need help to …
I think it might be unsuitable for …

Exam help

- ✓ Read the question carefully and plan your review before you start to write. Think of the style you will use, which will probably be semi-formal.
- ✓ Think about how you will organise the content. You need to deal with several tasks within the question: inform the reader about the programme and locations, give your personal opinion, and say if you think it is suitable for all ages.
- ✓ You will need to use varied language, including interesting adjectives. Avoid overusing words such as 'good' and 'nice'.
- ✓ Check your spelling and punctuation.

VISUALS BANK

Part 2 Candidate A

Here are your photographs. They show **people studying**. I'd like you to compare the photographs, and say **why the people have chosen to study in these places.**

Part 2 Candidate B

Here are your photographs. They show **people doing exercise**. I'd like you to compare the photographs, and say **how good these types of exercise might be for the people in the photos**.

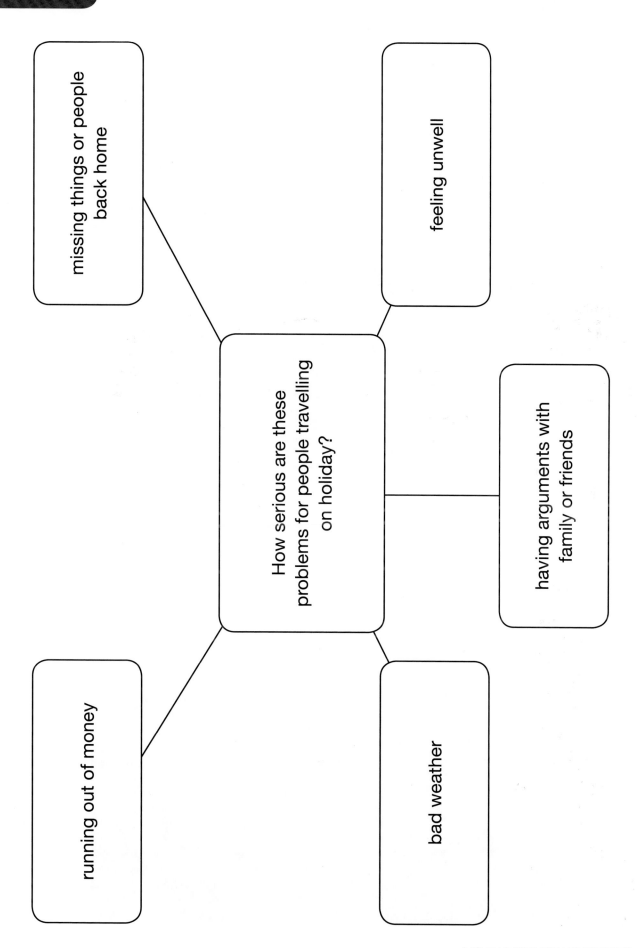

missing things or people back home

feeling unwell

How serious are these problems for people travelling on holiday?

having arguments with family or friends

running out of money

bad weather

Part 2 Candidate A

Here are your photographs. They show **people on holiday**. I'd like you to compare the photographs, and say **what type of person would choose these holidays**.

Here are your photographs. They show **people waiting**. I'd like you to compare the photographs, and say **how the people may be feeling**.

Part 3

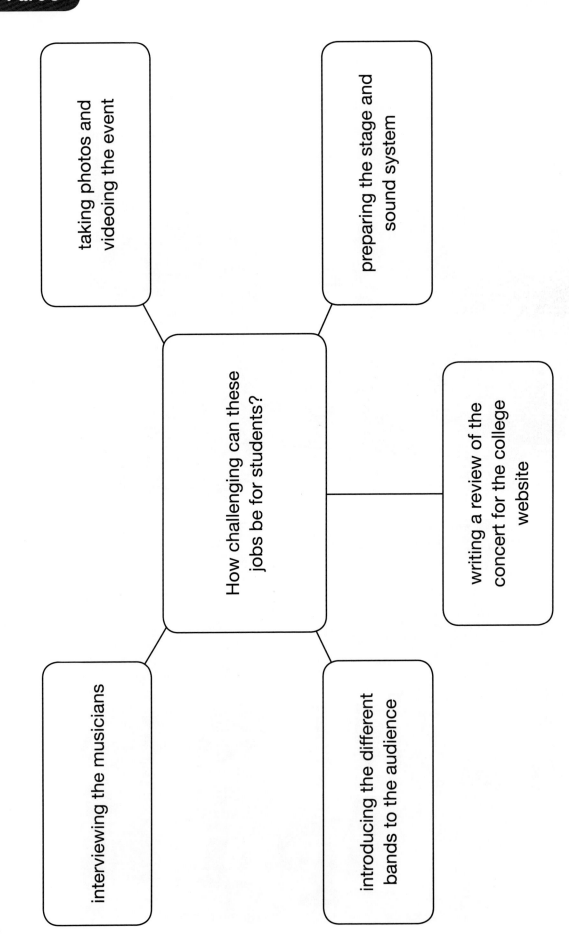

taking photos and videoing the event

preparing the stage and sound system

How challenging can these jobs be for students?

writing a review of the concert for the college website

interviewing the musicians

introducing the different bands to the audience

Here are your photographs. They show **people and animals**. I'd like you to compare the photographs, and say **how the people and the animals may be feeling**.

Part 2 Candidate B

They show **people playing different musical instruments**. I'd like you to compare the photographs, and say **how much the people may be enjoying the experience**.

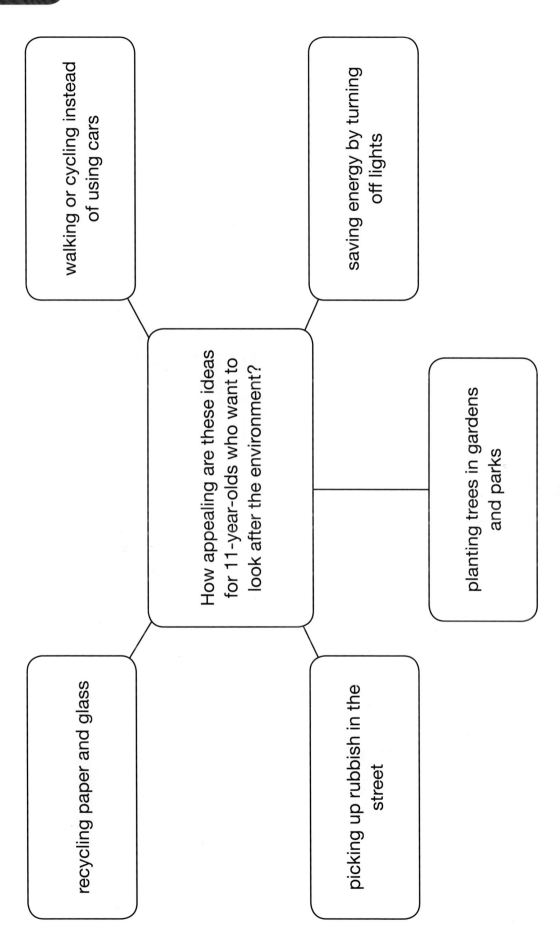

walking or cycling instead of using cars

saving energy by turning off lights

How appealing are these ideas for 11-year-olds who want to look after the environment?

planting trees in gardens and parks

recycling paper and glass

picking up rubbish in the street

Part 2 Candidate A

Here are your photographs. They show **people using different types of transport**. I'd like you to compare the photographs, and say **why the people may have chosen to travel in this way**.

They show people **playing different games**. I'd like you to compare the photographs, and say **how interesting these games would be for different age groups**.

Part 3

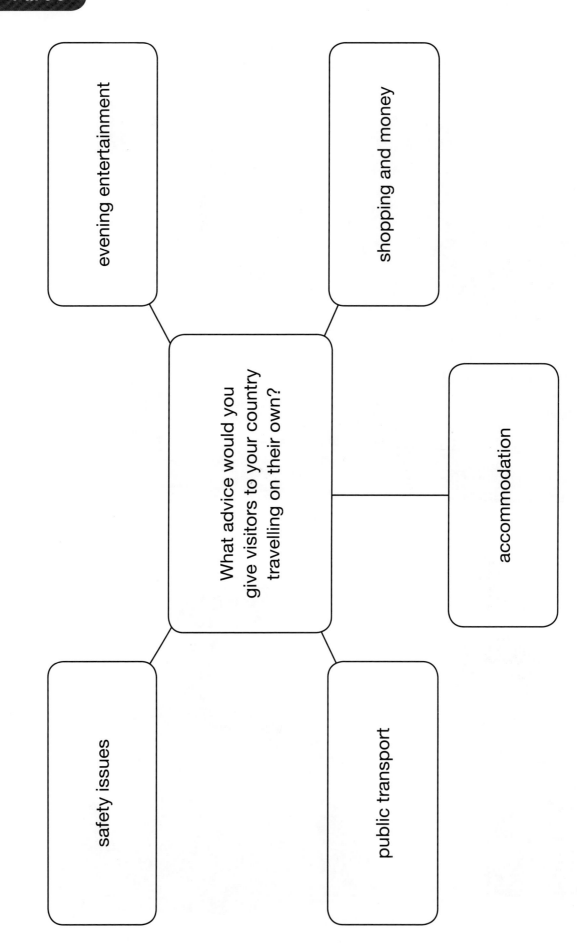

evening entertainment

shopping and money

What would you give visitors to your country travelling on their own?

accommodation

safety issues

public transport

Here are your photographs. They show **people taking a break**. I'd like you to compare the photographs, and say **why the people needed a break**.

Part 2 Candidate B

They show **people performing in front of an audience**. I'd like you to compare the photographs, and say **how the performers and the audience may be feeling**.

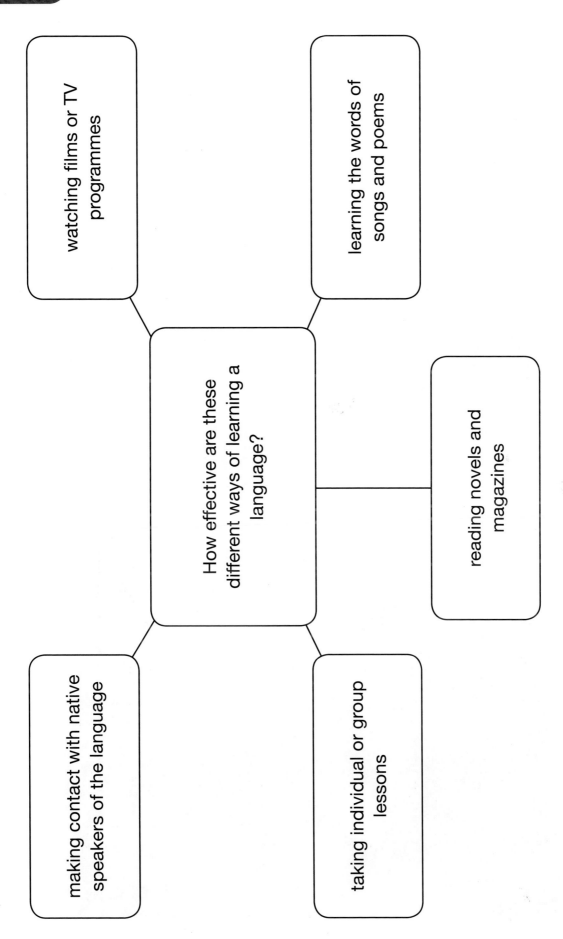

watching films or TV programmes

learning the words of songs and poems

How effective are these different ways of learning a language?

reading novels and magazines

making contact with native speakers of the language

taking individual or group lessons

Part 2 Candidate A

Here are your photographs. They show **people communicating in different ways**. I'd like you to compare the photographs, and say **how necessary it is for the people to communicate in these ways**.

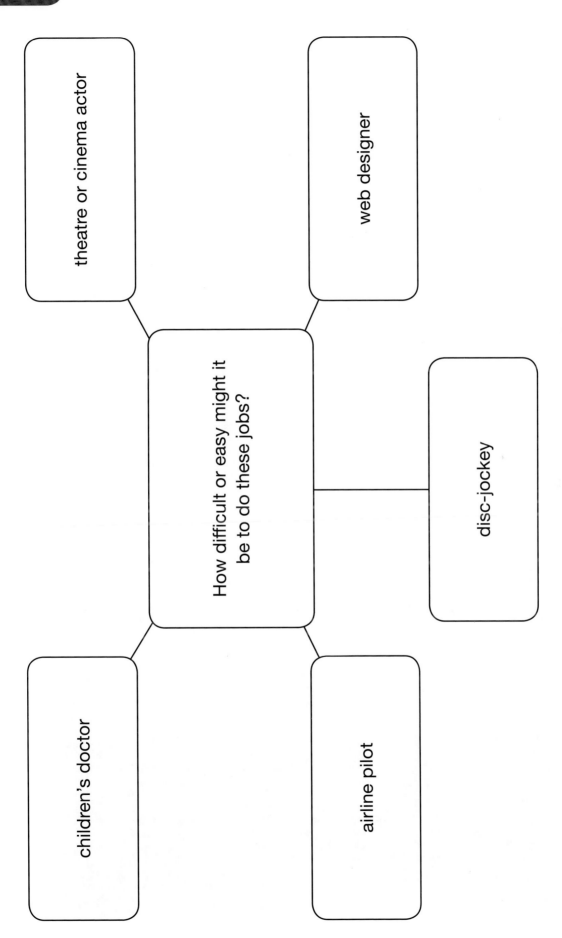

theatre or cinema actor

web designer

How difficult or easy might it be to do these jobs?

disc-jockey

children's doctor

airline pilot

Here are your photographs. They show **people taking part in competitions**. I'd like you to compare the photographs, and say **how the people may be feeling**.

Here are your photographs. They show **people paying attention**. I'd like you to compare the photographs, and say **why it's important to pay attention in these situations**.

TEST
7

VISUALS FOR
SPEAKING TESTS

Here are your photographs. They show **people meeting friends in different places**. I'd like you to compare the photographs, and say **why the friends may have chosen these places to meet**.

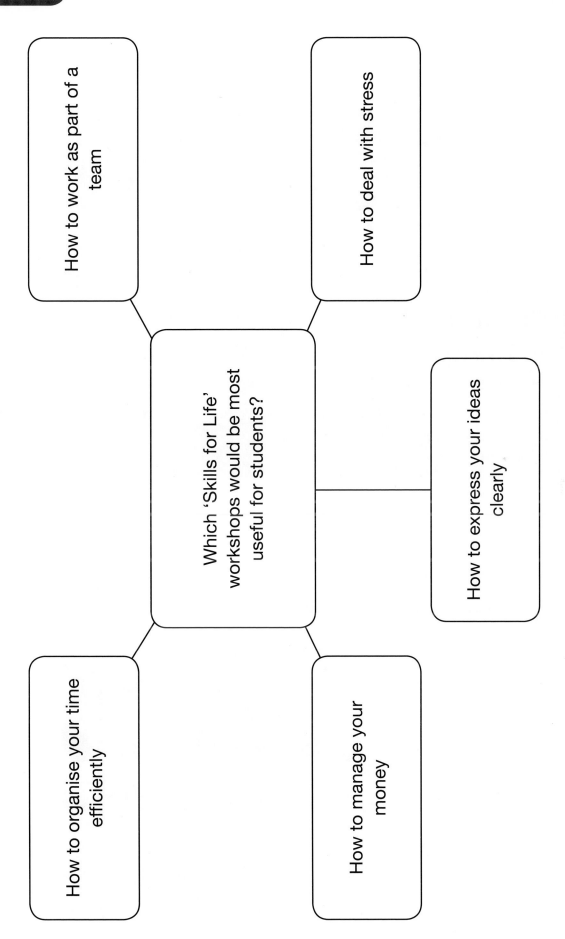

How to work as part of a team

How to deal with stress

Which 'Skills for Life' workshops would be most useful for students?

How to express your ideas clearly

How to organise your time efficiently

How to manage your money

Part 2 Candidate A

Here are your photographs. They show **people getting ready for something**. I'd like you to compare the photographs, and say **how the people might be feeling**.

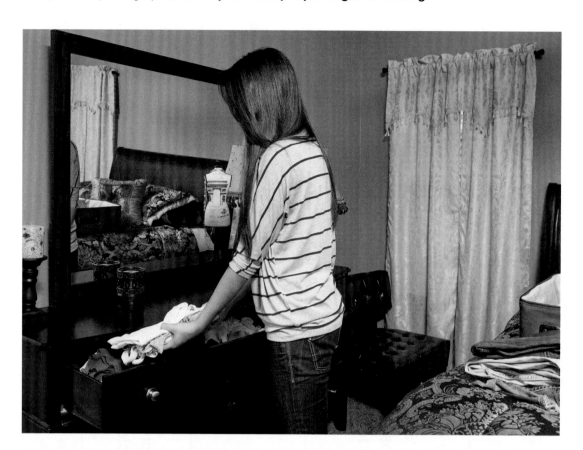

Here are your photographs. They show **people listening**. I'd like you to compare the photographs, and say **how important it is for the people to listen carefully**.

Part 3

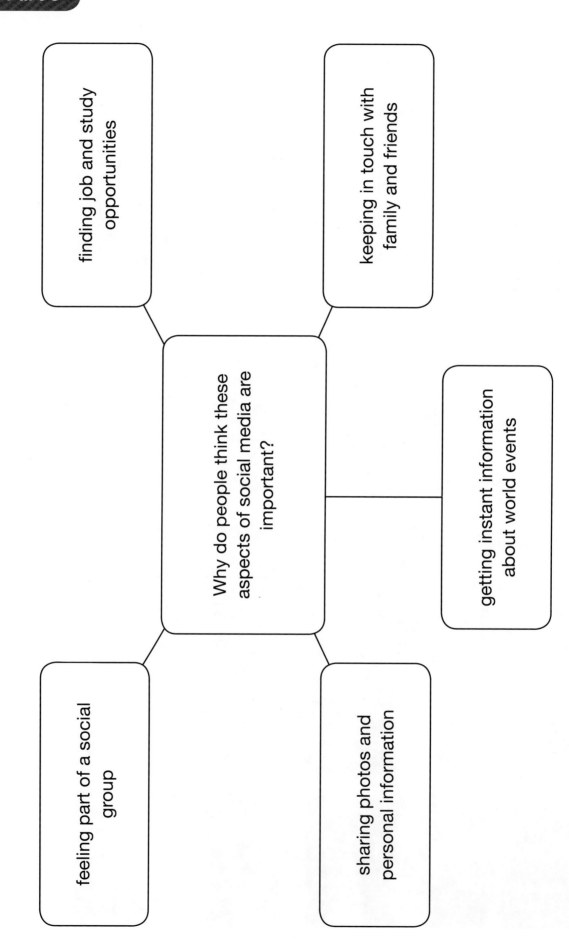

finding job and study
opportunities

keeping in touch with
family and friends

Why do people think these
aspects of social media are
important?

getting instant information
about world events

feeling part of a social
group

sharing photos and
personal information

ANSWER KEY

Part 1: Don't forget your hat

1   A: 'does the job' is a fixed phrase.
2   B: 'sending out' matches the meaning of 'lost' in the next sentence.
3   D: The other words don't give the idea of quantity.
4   C: The other words aren't followed by the preposition 'on'.
5   D: The other words can't be followed by 'you' + 'warm'.
6   C: The other words aren't usually used to talk about sunlight.
7   A: The other three words would need a new subject.
8   D: The other three words can't be followed by the adjective 'sunburnt'.

Part 2: Penguins on the move

9   which: (relative pronoun) introduces a clause
10   off: (preposition) part of the phrasal verb 'to show off'
11   since: part of the adverbial phrase 'ever since' meaning from that time until now
12   as: (adverbial) part of the linking phrase 'as if'
13   however: (linker) makes a contrast
14   in: part of the fixed phrase 'in search of'
15   is: (verb) part of passive construction meaning 'people think'
16   have: (auxiliary verb) part of compound tense

Part 3: The sky at night

17   mountainous: noun to adjective
18   pollution: verb to noun
19   fortunate: noun to adjective
20   impressive: verb to adjective
21   height: adjective to noun
22   uninterrupted: adjective to negative adjective
23   powerful: noun to adjective
24   discovery: verb to noun

Part 4

25   is being opened: passive form
26   looking forward to: fixed expression
27   been my intention to: verb to noun
28   didn't/did not mean to damage: fixed negative expression
29   to play tennis unless Fiona: infinitive after reporting verb, position of 'unless'
30   is expected to arrive: passive form

Part 5: Driving in the desert

31   D: She wanted to prove she could adapt to new situations.
32   B: 'same goals and same way of working.'
33   D: 'this' refers to the previous sentence.
34   B: 'the thing that scared us most.'
35   C: 'It's ... the people you least expect who help you most.'
36   A: 'they're less good at anticipating problems.'

Part 6: Music to get fit by

37   G: 'up your workout productivity by as much as 20 per cent' is an example of 'increased level of output'.
38   A: 'this word' refers to 'disassociation'.
39   C: 'one of them' refers back to 'there are some rules'.
40   F: 'he' refers to the writer's 'friend' and we read about the 'mistake' he made.
41   D: There is a link between 'songs' and 'limited number of them' and also between 'complaint' and 'This is because ...'.
42   B: 'golfers' serve as an example of the 'diverse range of sports'.

Part 7: Why do people start writing blogs?

43   D: 'a useful tool in my future job'
44   A: 'my blog is a business tool'
45   C: 'not the thing to do if you want to remain anonymous'
46   B: 'I needed to get some good content ...'
47   C: 'If I make mistakes I learn from ...'
48   A: 'I felt confident that I already knew ...'
49   B: 'I was basically a nobody'
50   D: 'Writing a 750 word article is ...'
51   C: 'refreshing to be able to step outside ...'
52   A: 'they kept them hidden under their beds'

Test 1: Writing (page 17)

Part 1

Question 1 (essay)

Style: formal

Content: **General:** answer the question about whether we can live happily without using things like phones and computers all the time, with examples and reasons for all your opinions.
  1 the technology we can't live without
  2 why to use or not to use phones in certain social situations
  3 another point to support your answer (different from 1 and 2)

Part 2

Question 2 (article)

Style: neutral or semi-formal

Content: describe your friend, the activities you did together, and explain why you got on well.

Question 3 (letter)

Style: Formal

Content: 1 explain that you are energetic and sociable, interested in the job and available in August
  2 explain that you are confident your level of fluency in English is high enough
  3 say you get on well with teenagers and give examples to prove it

Question 4 (report)

Style: neutral or semi-formal

Content: 1 say whether the facilities for popular sports, such as tennis courts or swimming pool, are good or not
  2 say whether the staff at the Reception desk and the sports trainers were helpful and welcoming
  3 mention the prices and say whether you think they are reasonable, in general and for students

Test 1: Listening (page 20)

Part 1

1	B	2	B	3	B	4	C
5	A	6	C	7	C	8	A

Part 2: Sailing solo across the Atlantic

9 5,600/five thousand, six hundred
10 *Cheeky Monkey*
11 (large/big) ships
12 tins
13 (hot) toast
14 binoculars
15 iPod
16 flying fish
17 Children in Need
18 photo(graph)s

Part 3

19 C	20 F	21 A	22 E	23 D

Part 4

24 B	25 B	26 C	27 C
28 A	29 B	30 A	

ANSWER KEY

Test 2: Reading and Use of English (page 28)

Part 1: Sudoku

1 C: Only the answer fits the sense of the sentence.
2 D: 'calls for' is a phrasal verb that means 'requires'.
3 A: 'general knowledge' is a common collocation.
4 B: 'work hard' is a common collocation.
5 B: 'taken off' is a phrasal verb which means 'become a success'.
6 C: 'benefit' is followed by the preposition 'from'.
7 B: Only 'regard' can be followed by a phrase with 'it as'.
8 A: Only the correct answer creates a contrast in this position in the sentence.

Part 2: The Birth of *YouTube*

9   how: (determiner) gives the idea of degree
10 with: (preposition) to 'come up with' is a phrasal verb which means to have a new idea
11 set: (verb) 'set up' is a phrasal verb that means establish – it collocates with 'a business'
12 would/might: (modal verb) part of reported speech after 'thought'
13 than: (conjunction) 'more than' tells us the size of a number
14 on: (preposition) collocates with the word 'average'
15 which: (relative pronoun) links two parts of the sentence
16 other: (adverbial) 'in other words' is a fixed expression which introduces an explanation

Part 3: Putting the fun back into driving

17 pleasure: verb to noun
18 growth: verb to noun
19 safety: adjective to noun
20 introduction: verb to noun
21 performance: verb to noun
22 informal: adjective to negative adjective
23 popularity: adjective to noun
24 variety: verb to noun

Part 4

25 wasn't/was not as difficult: comparative with adverbial phrase
26 advised Leon to tell: reported speech + infinitive
27 a small number of people: way of expressing quantity
28 took part in: fixed phrase
29 as long as you're/you are: conditional form
30 (that) she'd/she had chosen: 'wish' + past perfect

Part 5: Extract from a Novel

31 B: 'I was really impressed with the place initially, thinking we'd finally found the true countryside.'
32 A: '… the place wasn't quite what it seemed anyway. The only field that went with the farmhouse was the one beside the track.'
33 C: 'The bedrooms were huge, but they hardly had any furniture in them.'
34 B: 'She asked if we were on holiday, and I listened with interest to my aunt's answer. I don't think I really understood at that point what she was doing.'
35 C: 'it' refers back to the word 'each', which is talking about the photographs – so it refers to one of the photographs.
36 D: 'Also it was clear that you didn't have to pay for it, so I realised it couldn't be up to much.'

Part 6: Bottlenose whales

37 A: 'from a distance' before the gap links to 'When you come closer' in A.
38 F: 'these basic facts' in F refers to the size and weight of the whales mentioned before the gap.
39 G: There is a link between 'sound' before the gap and 'these strange noises in G: also the 'four creatures' in G are referred to by 'the smallest one' after the gap.
40 C: 'heads all pointing our way' before the gap links to 'watching us' in C, which is also referred to by 'being studied' after the gap.
41 E: 'making a huge splash' in E is an example of a 'way to be heard' before the gap.
42 B: 'This revelation' after the gap refers to 'a depth of nine hundred metres' in B.

Part 7: Female referees and umpires

43 A: 'I made sure I was on top of every detail of the game so that I couldn't make a wrong decision.'
44 D: '(men's rugby) players like having me as a ref because they can hear my voice. They can pick it out more easily than they could a male voice in the heat of the match.'
45 C: An umpire's performance is assessed in all international matches, and they have to score a minimum 8 out of 10 every time to keep their position.
46 C: '… such things as signalling clearly to the other umpire on the pitch …'
47 A: 'some people did have that "what would she know about football?" attitude. But once they saw me on the field, refereeing a match, they soon changed their tune.'

48 B: By doing TV talk shows and other public appearances, she's hoping to open doors so that others can follow in her footsteps.

49 B: 'I don't think that it's widely appreciated what it means to work at professional games day in, day out, always on the road.'

50 D: When Grace Gavin heard that her application to become a rugby referee had been accepted, she was in a taxi. 'I was completely taken aback.'

51 B: '…the one group of people I haven't had a single problem with are the male players, coaches or managers. If anything, they tend to be even more respectful to me than they'd usually be.'

52 A: She's soft-spoken and appears shy and unassuming, in sharp contrast to how she is on the field, where she comes across as loud and aggressive.

Test 2: Writing (page 39)

Part 1

Question 1 (essay)

Style: formal

Content: **General**: agree or disagree with the idea that friends are for good times as well as for bad times, with examples and reasons for all your opinions.

1 what friends can do when you need help and advice

2 how friends can have a good time together

3 another point to support your answer (different from 1 and 2)

Part 2

Question 2 (email)

Style: informal

Content: 1 inexpensive/free music events available

2 visits to museums and reasons for choices

3 how to make the most of the time

Question 3 (review)

Style: semi-formal or neutral.

Content: 1 describe the programme (both content and locations) and say why it is interesting

2 explain why you think the programme is (un)suitable for children, teenagers and/or adults

Question 4 (article)

Style: formal or neutral

Content: 1 explain how you met the person who became so important to you

2 explain why he or she became so important

3 describe how your relationship developed since then

Test 2: Listening (page 42)

Part 1

1	A	2	C	3	B	4	A
5	C	6	A	7	B	8	B

Part 2: The Loch Ness Monster

9 sheep
10 surgeon's
11 boat
12 fine/good
13 publicity
14 photography
15 submarine
16 dolphins
17 flipper
18 plants/animals (in either order)

Part 3

19 H	20 C	21 A	22 D	23 B

Part 4

24 C	25 A	26 B	27 B
28 C	29 A	30 C	

Test 3: Reading and Use of English (page 50)

Part 1: Boots for Africa

1 C: The correct answer creates the multi-word verb 'joined forces' which means cooperated with.
2 B: Only the correct answer can be followed by 'as'.
3 D: Only the correct answer fits the meaning of the sentence.
4 A: The other words can't be can't be followed by the preposition 'in'.
5 C: Only the correct answer collocates with 'good'.
6 A: Only the correct answer fits the meaning of the sentence.
7 D: The other words don't collocate with 'donation'.
8 B: The other words don't collocate with 'information'.

Part 2: An influential cook

9 for: (preposition) indicates a period of time
10 been: (auxiliary verb) passive form
11 rather: (adverb) part of the comparative linker 'rather than'
12 when: (relative pronoun) indicates a time clause
13 which/that: (relative pronoun) introduces a clause
14 more: (adverb) part of the linker 'what's more'
15 at: (preposition) part of the quantifier 'at least'
16 in: (preposition) used before 'number'

Part 3: Young artists on display

17 exhibition: verb to noun
18 traditionally: noun to adverb
19 tourists: noun to plural noun
20 wonderful: noun to adjective
21 pride: adjective to noun
22 favourite/favorite: verb to adjective
23 effective: verb to adjective
24 enthusiastic: noun to adjective

Part 4

25 off in case David: phrasal verb + 'in case' + subject
26 were given a map by: passive voice + agent
27 told me not to touch: reported speech + infinitive
28 a (much) faster typist: comparative adjective + 'than'
29 is unlikely to last: passive form + infinitive
30 has difficulty (in) answering: noun phrase + gerund

Part 5: Travelling to learn

31 B: 'Three years later . . . my conversational skills were limited.'
32 B: 'but two little words have always stopped me: home stay.'
33 C: 'thinking, 'What have I let myself in for?''
34 A: 'one of us is a bit alarmed . . . another is disconcerted.'
35 D: 'wondering if they'll be able to cope.'
36 C: 'We take it in turns to pluck up the courage to ring our 'Mums' and ask if we can stay out late – rather strange when you consider that our average age is probably thirty-three.'

Part 6: If you're happy the robot knows it

37 B: Link between 'the user changes position' and 'when you hang your head and . . .'.
38 G: Link between 'its creators' and 'they'. Link between 'people' and them'.
39 D: Link between 'is nothing new' and 'researchers . . . have already proved . . .'.
40 A: Link between 'foster greater attention' and 'provoke a greater response'. Link between the question and 'To find out, . . .'.
41 F: Link between 'influence over the volunteers' and 'actually prompted lots of participants'.
42 E: Link between 'not universally accepted' and 'cannot protect the group' and 'this can be resolved'.

Part 7: Wild camping

43 B: '. . . the excitement that comes from making yourself slightly vulnerable'
44 C: 'In less paranoid times, . . . but people nowadays . . .'
45 C: 'not keen to suggest good places . . .'
46 D: 'managed to pass on some of my enthusiasm'
47 A: 'people need to ask themselves: 'Do I really need this?' before packing their stuff.'
48 B: 'the memory of that put me off wild camping for months'
49 A: 'are waking up to the fact . . .'
50 D: 'somebody had failed to extinguish a small fire'
51 C: 'I'd advise places which aren't too far from civilisation'
52 A: 'you can seldom escape the constant chattering . . . or, worse still . . .'

Test 3: Writing (page 60)

Part 1

Question 1 (essay)

Style: formal

Content: **General**: say whether you agree or disagree with the idea that the only way to learn about the world is to travel, with examples and reasons for all your opinions.

  1 how important it is to see how people live in other countries

  2 whether it is possible to learn about the world by reading or watching things on the internet

  3 another point to support your answer (different from 1 and 2)

Part 2

Question 2 (article)

Style: formal or neutral

Content: 1 describe your favourite sport

  2 say at what age and why you started, who you played with

  3 say how it would help people make new friends

Question 3 (email)

Style: informal

Content: 1 say what the summer job is, and how much or how little you like it

  2 explain whether you find it difficult / easy to work when other people are on holiday

  3 say how much your free time you get, and whether you earn enough

Question 4 (report)

Style: neutral or semi-formal

Content: 1 describe some of the dishes you learnt to cook

  2 say whether you found the course useful or not and why

  3 say whether you would recommend it to beginners of all ages and why

Test 3: Listening (page 62)

Part 1

1	A	2	B	3	A	4	C
5	A	6	A	7	C	8	B

Part 2: History of roller skating

9 Holland

10 violin

11 (large) mirror

12 *Winter Pleasures*

13 direction

14 (roller) hockey

15 championships

16 design/performance (in either order)

17 eight million/8,000,000

18 lighter/safer (in either order)

Part 3

19 D	20 B	21 C	22 A	23 F

Part 4

24 B	25 C	26 A	27 B
28 C	29 C	30 A	

Test 4: Reading and Use of English (page 68)

Part 1: Lunch is for Sharing

1 C: The answer is the correct term in the context of websites.
2 B: The other words don't collocate with 'record'.
3 C: The other words can't be followed by 'of'.
4 D: The other words can't be followed by 'as'.
5 A: The others words can't be followed by 'of'.
6 B: The other words can't be used after 'in.
7 A: The other words do not make sense in the context.
8 B: 'health conscious' is a common collocation.

Part 2: Mr Bean

9 more (quantifier): 'more than' indicates a larger quantity
10 well (adjective): part of comparative phrase
11 (Al)though/while/whilst (linker): introduces a contrastive clause
12 to (preposition): part of fixed expression indicating opinion
13 his (pronoun): 'own' with this meaning always has a personal pronoun.
14 who (relative pronoun): introduces a clause
15 around (preposition): links idea to personal pronoun
16 such (adverbial): part of fixed expression used to indicate an example

Part 3: Computer Games

17 influential: noun to adjective
18 creative: verb to adjective
19 impressive: verb to adjective
20 development: verb to noun
21 similarity: adjective to noun
22 economists: noun to plural noun
23 explanation: verb to noun
24 unexpected: adjective to negative adjective

Part 4

25 the most interesting place: change of form of adjective and syntax
26 flight had been on time: conditional with past perfect
27 not read your email unless: negative verb plus 'unless'
28 wishes she had not lent: past perfect after 'wish'
29 must/will have been really disappointed: passive form with adjective
30 turned down Alex's: phrasal verb with possessive form of name

Part 5: Extract from a novel

31 C: 'The things you worry about don't always turn out as badly as you expect. Sometimes they're worse.'
32 B: 'I'd got a special cheap offer on the Internet. But that was silly because Ruth's aunt was paying our expenses.'
33 A: 'gripping the pen hard so that my name wouldn't look as shaky as I felt'
34 D: 'You just need to follow the coast road,' said Ruth. 'It's simple …'.
35 B: 'lights would blaze round a corner ahead, without warning, looking as though they were coming right at us'
36 C: 'Ruth read out where I should go '… just like the directions say.'

Part 6: Femi Kuti, a great African musician

37 C: Link between 'his father' and 'his father's long shadow. 'Link between 'a fine performer in his own right' and 'bringing his own unique creativity'.
38 F: Link between 'his son' and 'giving him'. Link between 'any signs of approval' and 'refused to give him lessons'.
39 A: Link between 'failed to make it on to the plane' and 'fill his place'. Link between 'did so … with considerable skill' and 'This gave him the confidence …'.
40 E: Link between 'Femi's debut album' and 'Now a collector's item, its mix of …'.
41 B: Link between 'album … which earned him good reviews' and 'It also won …' Link between 'reconciliation with his father' and 'He finally admitted …'.
42 G: Link between 'he learnt things from him' and 'he taught me to be different'.

Part 7: Anyone for extreme sports?

43 B: '…I had forgotten my first important lesson'
44 D: 'returning to the sport might be like riding a bike'
45 A: 'I'd no doubt be able to take my body weight …'
46 B: 'I did so and my more relaxed style …'
47 B: 'I know I'll feel completely at ease eventually'
48 A: '…I noticed a slight fluttering in my stomach'
49 D: 'What a thrill to feel the cool air …'
50 C: '…isn't so risky. When practised correctly …'
51 C: 'My partner … had trouble …Then I dived … reached … easily'
52 A: 'a real feeling of regret when the instructor told me to drop.'

Test 4: Writing (page 78)

Part 1

Question 1 (essay)

Style: formal

Content: **General**: say whether you agree or disagree with the idea that people should do a job they love and not worry about money, with examples and reasons for all your opinions.

1 the importance of being happy with the job you do

2 the need to earn money to support yourself or a family

3 another point to support your answer (different from 1 and 2)

Part 2

Question 2 (letter)

Style: Formal

Content: 1 give reasons why you want to attend the course

2 mention any musical skills you have

3 give details about your favourite type of music

Question 3 (review)

Style: semi-formal or neutral.

Content: 1 describe the cartoon and some of the characters

2 explain why it makes you laugh

3 say why it may or may not appeal to older people

Question 4 (article)

Style: formal or neutral

Content: 1 describe the job you wanted to do in the future when you were a child, saying why it seemed the ideal job then

2 explain how you changed your mind as you grew older

Test 4: Listening (page 80)

Part 1

1	C	2	C	3	B	4	C
5	B	6	C	7	A	8	A

Part 2: Rita Lewis: TV researcher

9 biology

10 media studies

11 Costa Rica

12 twelve/12

13 (poisonous) frog

14 (thirty-metre high) waterfall

15 tuna

16 torch

17 sun(-)gun

18 scared

Part 3

19 G	20 D	21 F	22 A	23 E

Part 4

24 A	25 B	26 B	27 C
28 A	29 C	30 B	

Part 1:   The world's finest chocolates

1	B:	The other words don't make sense in the context.
2	A:	Only the correct answer makes sense in the context.
3	C:	The other word don't collocate with 'thought'.
4	B:	'Picking up' is a phrasal verb which means 'collecting'.
5	C:	Only the correct answer can be followed by the preposition 'in'.
6	D:	The other options can't be used with 'than'.
7	C:	The other words don't collocate with 'selection'.
8	A:	The other words don't collocate with 'close up'.

Part 2:   Health on holiday

9 a/any/much: (quantifier) to indicate degree
10 is: (verb) follows the main subject of the sentence
11 that/which: (relative pronoun) introduces further information about the kit
12 on/forth: (preposition) completes the expression meaning 'et cetera'
13 out: (preposition) 'sorted out' is a phrasal verb meaning 'solved'
14 what: (determiner) links two infinitives
15 how: (determiner) means 'in what way'
16 case: (noun) completes the linking phrase 'in case'

Part 3:   Music and maths

17	performances:	verb to plural noun
18	movement:	verb to noun
19	endless:	noun to adjective
20	connection:	verb to noun
21	references:	verb to plural noun
22	fascination:	verb to noun
23	relationship:	concrete noun to abstract noun
24	unexpected:	verb to negative adjective

Part 4

25 was the first time (that): past tense plus common expression
26 from Luca, all (of): preposition plus positive idea
27 has no objection to: collocation plus noun from verb
28 is supposed to be: passive form
29 was not allowed while/whilst: passive voice plus time reference
30 if the machine had been: third conditional with past perfect tense

Part 5:   The Cranston Institute of Modern Music

31	B:	We're more band, more rock'n'roll oriented.
32	A:	The information about contracts in the next sentence supports this.
33	D:	'...the main thing for me is the live performance events.'
34	C:	This is supported by the fact that they didn't 'engage with school'.
35	C:	'It's a bit like a football team here, with people fulfilling different roles.'
36	B:	'many' (of them) are the tutors mentioned in the previous sentence.

Part 6:   What is cryptozoology?

37	E:	Link between 'them' and the animals listed before the gap. Link between 'them' and 'they're' after the gap.
38	G:	Link between 'interested me more' and the subjects listed before the gap. Link between 'romantic aspects' and the film.
39	D:	Link between 'the animal itself' and 'snakeskin' before the gap. Link between 'the animal itself' and 'I didn't find one' after the gap.
40	C:	Link between 'these' and 'fakes' before the gap. Link between 'one percent' and 'a much higher figure' after the gap'.
41	F:	Link between 'with it' and the statue mentioned before the gap.
42	A:	Link between 'members' and the two groups mentioned before the gap. ' and 'these' after the gap.

Part 7:   What sort of person do you need to be work in tourism?

43	B:	'There's a shortage of first-class chefs'
44	C:	'allow people to do what they want, ... at the same time making sure ...'
45	B:	'Had I taken a full-time college course ... I would have ...'
46	D:	'It's crucial to be able to exercise good judgement ...'
47	A:	'not to be put off by ... low wages at the start'
48	B:	'though these advantages are more likely to come from ...'
49	A:	'the right degree ... is no guarantee ...'
50	C:	'a holidaymaker spotted some incorrect details ...'
51	D:	'educational institutions are beginning to ...'
52	E:	'The recruitment outlook isn't very promising right now ...'

Test 5: Writing (page 96)

Part 1

Question 1 (essay)

Style: formal

Content: **General**: answer the question about why many young people want to follow the latest fashion in clothes and hair styles, with examples and reasons for all your opinions.

1 young people may want to imitate celebrities they admire

2 young people may feel they have to follow certain fashions to feel accepted

3 another point to support your answer (different from 1 and 2)

Part 2

Question 2 (letter)

Style: Formal

Content: 1 say in what ways you are good at working with people

2 describe your level of English, and of any other languages you know

3 say you can work flexible hours

4 give any other reasons why you would be suitable for this job

Question 3 (review)

Style: semi-formal or neutral.

Content: 1 describe some of the characters in the soap opera and say why they are interesting

2 say why you watch it regularly

3 explain why you would or would not recommend it to everyone

Question 4 (email)

Style: informal

Content: 1 say whether sport is important in the life of young people in your country

2 describe the main sports they do and say whether sport is part of college life

3 mention the names of any sports personalities in your country that young people admire

Test 5: Listening (page 98)

Part 1

1	C	2	C	3	C	4	B
5	C	6	A	7	B	8	C

Part 2: The peacock

9 fan

10 India

11 four thousand/4,000

12 neck

13 eyes

14 brown

15 proud

16 water

17 sleep

18 crocodiles

Part 3

19	E	20	B	21	F	22	C	23	H

Part 4

24	C	25	B	26	A	27	B
28	A	29	A	30	C

Test 6: Reading and Use of English (page 104)

Part 1: My first expedition

1. B: You can't use the preposition 'by' before the other words.
2. B: The other words can't modify 'not'.
3. C: The other words don't collocate with 'moment'.
4. A: 'drop out' is a phrasal verb that means 'withdraw from a commitment'.
5. D: Only the correct answer collocates with 'notice' to form the common expression.
6. A: The other words don't collocate with 'doubts'.
7. A: The other words don't make sense in the context.
8. C: Only the correct answer makes sense in context.

Part 2: Shopping trolley joins the push for fitness

9. what: (determiner) part of the expression 'what is called'
10. which: (relative pronoun) introduces more information about the trolley
11. into: (preposition) the verb 'transform' is followed by this preposition
12. and: (conjunction) completes the idea begun with 'both'
13. are: (verb) passive voice
14. with: (preposition) introduces additional information
15. other: (adjective) part of fixed linking expression
16. out: (preposition) To point out is a phrasal verb meaning to inform

Part 3: Toy story

17. carefully: adjective to adverb
18. collection: verb to noun
19. appearance: verb to noun
20. outfits: verb to plural compound noun
21. variety: verb to noun
22. undamaged: adjective to negative adjective
23. investment: verb to noun
24. impressive: verb to adjective

Part 4

25. as a surprise to Pete: fixed expression
26. are not as serious as: comparative form
27. was still doing/finishing: positive continuous verb form with 'still'
28. were you, I would make: conditional form plus phrase instead of verb
29. my opinion it was: opinion plus new subject
30. been living in Toronto since: present continuous plus preposition

Part 5: Assistants to the stars

31: B: 'he was initially reluctant to talk to me because I was a journalist.'
32: C: 'were still widely sought after …'
33: A: 'he's looking to unwind in front of the television after a long day's work.'
34: C: 'Without wasting another minute, he sets about searching for the contact details of the four assistants on the show.'
35: B: 'was extremely courageous – there's no denying that.'
36: D: 'being an assistant was not the means to an end but an end in itself.'

Part 6: Cayman Brac and Little Cayman

37. E: Link between 'lovers of the outdoors' and 'They'. Link between 'outdoors' and 'walking and cycling'. Link between 'diving' and 'divers'.
38. F: Link between 'not really built up apart from …' and 'this lack of development'.
39. A: Link between 'coral reef' and 'It starts … and plunges'.
40. D: Link between 'not just about the sea' and 'back on land'.
41. G: Link between 'is quite different', 'it is much livelier' and 'The locals are friendly'.
42. B: Link between 'migrant birds' and 'As well as these visitors'.

Part 7: The bestsellers

43. A: 'This shop's also an information centre'
44. B: 'making his shop window eye-catching … It is … important.'
45. C: 'sat in cafés and listened to conversations …'
46. B: 'the people … helping the customer … don't feel they're valued'
47. D: 'I was having a conversation … I said I'd have …'
48. A: 'We carry a vast range … show children the world …'
49. B: 'mostly university students and young professionals'
50. C: 'I've got a pretty good idea of what's in most of them'
51. D: 'a space upstairs for author talks and …'
52. A: 'buyers from the area are loyal …'

Test 6: Writing (page 114)

Part 1

Question 1 (essay)

Style: formal

Content: **General**: say whether you agree or disagree with the idea that you must live in a town if you want to study, work and have fun; with examples and reasons for all your opinions.

1. a town or city offers a variety of opportunities for education, work and leisure
2. internet facilities make it possible to work and study from home in the countryside
3. another point to support your answer (different from 1 and 2)

Part 2

Question 2 (letter)

Style: Formal

Content: 1. say which team you would like to join and why
2. mention any experience you have of that particular area
3. say when you would be able to start

Question 3 (review)

Style: semi-formal or neutral.

Content: 1. comment on the songs
2. describe and give an opinion about the performers
3. say whether the college hall is a good venue and give reasons

Question 4 (email)

Style: informal

Content: 1. advantages and/or disadvantages of spending the money on different types of books and magazines
2. advantages and/or disadvantages of spending the money on computers
3. conclusions and advice for the chief librarian

Test 6: Listening (page 116)

Part 1

1	C	2	A	3	C	4	C
5	C	6	B	7	B	8	B

Part 2: The carbon coach

9. consultant
10. ecologist
11. bills
12. carbon meter
13. (the) government
14. light bulbs
15. (its/their) concerts
16. earth(-)ship
17. (the) wind (power)
18. handbook

Part 3

19 E	20 F	21 A	22 B	23 D

Part 4

24 B	25 A	26 B	27 C
28 C	29 B	30 A	

Test 7: Reading and Use of English (page 122)

Part 1: Baseball caps

1 B: The other words can't be followed by 'with'.
2 B: The answer completes the common collocation 'keep out of'.
3 A: The other words don't collocate well with 'thing'.
4 D: The other words aren't followed by 'to'.
5 A: To 'catch on' is a phrasal verb meaning to become popular.
6 D: The other words can't be followed by 'that'.
7 C: The other words aren't followed by 'of'.
8 B: The other words don't collocate with 'thanks'.

Part 2: Unemployed elephants

9   however: (linker) creates a contrast
10 in: (preposition) collocates with 'decline'
11 rather: (adverbial) completes the contrastive linking expression with 'than'
12 need: (verb) completes the common expression
13 with: (preposition) collocates with 'provide'
14 as: (adverbial) collocates with 'regarded'
15 who: (relative pronoun) introduces a clause
16 much: (adjective) completes the comparative expression to indicate quantity

Part 3: Bananas

17 natural: noun to adjective
18 tasty: noun to adjective
19 successful: noun to adjective
20 coastal: noun to adjective
21 constantly: adjective to adverb
22 unprotected: verb to negative adjective
23 treatment: verb to noun
24 distribution: verb to noun

Part 4

25 given up trying: phrasal verb plus gerund
26 used to play a lot: 'used to' plus infinitive
27 was not able to swim: negative verb plus preposition
28 him to make sure (that): direct to reported speech
29 run out of: phrasal verb
30 is trying to keep: present continuous tense plus collocation

Part 5: Extract from a novel

31 A: '... my family were getting on my nerves'
32 A: The pronoun refers directly back to the last noun.
33 D: 'submerged rocks ... which made landing too risky.'
34 B: This expression is used in the context of disappointment.
35 D: 'by the time he looked ... it had gone'
36 C: 'after that I couldn't pay attention to anything else.'

Part 6: Making special effects for the film *The Fountain*

37 D: Link between 'one day he called my studio ... the film was back on again' and 'There was one condition, though ...'.
38 G: Link between 'sample special effects ... thought had been wasted effort' and 'this unused material'.
39 A: Link between 'avoid the unrealistic ... depictions of space' and 'something more lifelike'.
40 E: Link between 'close-up shooting of very small things' and 'this method'. Link between 'fluid painting' and 'clear liquids'.
41 F: Link between 'I'd start with ... clear liquids ...' and 'I'd then add drops ...'. Link between 'liquids' and 'I use fluids ...'.
42 B: Link between 'surface of the sun' and 'the real solar surface'.

Part 7: The 'Gap Year': experiencing new sights, climates and cultures

43 B: 'I jumped at the chance of applying.'
44 A: 'Those who had were very obviously more mature.'
45 C: 'As well as working in an office ...'
46 B: 'you don't have to be brilliant at the sport.'
47 C: 'I learnt that I couldn't cook and that ...'
48 A: 'mention it when writing to prospective employers'
49 D: 'But I'd recommend going with somebody else'
50 A: 'provided I used the time to maximum advantage'
51 D: 'She suggested keeping a journal, which I did.'
52 C: 'I had to divide my gap year into two blocks'

Test 7: Writing (page 132)

Part 1

Question 1 (essay)

Style: formal

Content: **General:** say whether you agree or disagree with the idea that it is impossible to have a healthy lifestyle when you are studying or working hard, with examples and reasons for all your opinions.

1. the need to have the right balance between work and leisure
2. ways of finding time to cook and eat healthy food
3. another point to support your answer (different from 1 and 2)

Part 2

Question 2 (email)

Style: informal

Content:
1. confirm whether you are planning to take a year off after school
2. give information and opinions about possible trips available
3. give information and opinions about the possibility of doing voluntary work

Question 3 (review)

Style: semi-formal or neutral.

Content:
1. describe some of the things exhibited
2. say whether the information available was enough, well-presented, etc.
3. mention the facilities (e.g. sitting areas, café) and say what they were like

Question 4 (letter)

Style: Formal

Content:
1. say which course you would like to attend and give reasons
2. describe any experience you have had of organising events, for example at college

Test 7: Listening (page 134)

Part 1

1	C	2	C	3	A	4	C
5	A	6	B	7	A	8	B

Part 2: Mara Barnes: Surfer

9 exhausted
10 yoga
11 fourteen/14
12 nose
13 pollution
14 ears
15 Sunset Beach
16 meat/fish (in either order)
17 fruit
18 (a game of) chess

Part 3

19 D	20 F	21 B	22 H	23 C

Part 4

24 B	25 B	26 C	27 A
28 B	29 A	30 C	

Test 8: Reading and Use of English (page 140)

Part 1: Solar power

1 D: The other words don't make sense in the context.
2 C: The other words don't complete the common expression.
3 B: The other words don't make sense in the context.
4 A: The other words can't be followed by 'why'.
5 A: The other words aren't correct when talking about sunlight.
6 C: 'heats up' is a phrasal verb meaning 'gets hotter'.
7 B: The other words aren't followed by 'with'.
8 A: The other words aren't followed by 'on'.

Part 2: Online shopping

9 Despite: (linking adverb) introduces a contrastive clause
10 way: (noun)
11 as: (adverb) collocates with 'regard'
12 more: (comparative adjective) part of a fixed expression
13 on: (preposition) used with 'market'
14 come: (verb) collocates with 'decision'
15 one: (quantifier) used to give an example
16 few: (quantifier) qualifies a countable noun

Part 3: The blind pilot

17 amazing: verb to adjective
18 navigation: verb to noun
19 wonderful: verb to adjective
20 variety: verb to noun
21 unpleasant: adjective to negative adjective
22 frightening: noun to adjective
23 achievement: verb to noun
24 assistance: verb to noun

Part 4

25 necessary to fill in an: adjective plus phrasal verb
26 keep/stay dry even though: verb plus opposite adjective, plus linker
27 wish I could play: modal after 'I wish'
28 unless you pay by the: present tense after 'unless'
29 was fascinated by: change form of adjective
30 had bought her ticket: conditional with past perfect

Part 5: Pauline Koner

31 B: 'I couldn't express what I wanted in toe shoes.'
32 C: 'exhibited her unquestionable fight to stand alone.'
33 A: 'I was really living that way of dancing.'
34 B: 'she had already established herself.'

35 A: The word refers directly to the last noun in the previous sentence.
36 D: 'kindred spirit' means having the same ideas and approach to things.

Part 6: Making a boat into a home

37 B: Link between 'the barge was better …' and 'But you could … on the tugboat'. Link between 'the tugboat' and 'It was …'.
38 G: Link between 'below deck' and 'upstairs'. Link between 'accommodation' and 'This included a … kitchen …'.
39 E: Link between 'room at the back' and 'get the boat in there'. Link between 'get the boat in there' and 'fitted like a glove'.
40 A: Link between 'Adrian might like to do the work …' and 'He'd worked with wood …' Link between 'he'd' and 'Adrian had got tired …'.
41 F: Link between 'the worst job' and 'such a daunting task'. Link between 'daunting task' and 'paid a specialist to do it'.
42 C: Link between 'the boat moves too much' and 'feels as if it's … middle of the sea' and 'The tide produces …'.

Part 7: New kids on the frock

43 A: 'A lot of colleges are either one thing or the other … but we had a good mix.'
44 A: '… we felt like we were at the heart of everything – an important part of the city'
45 C: 'I've looked to knots in sailing for inspiration.'
46 D: 'I'm free from all the influences there, so I've developed my own style'
47 C: '… celebrity designer, and I have to admit … does appeal to me.'
48 B: '… the college's centenary year … I made my designs to reflect …'
49 A: '… there would be fewer social temptations there'
50 D: 'I wanted to use durable fabrics, so my collection includes a lot of leather'
51 B: 'great thing … feels like part of an art college … graphics and sculpture, too.'
52 B: 'My granny was a very glamorous model … gave me ideas.'

Test 8: Writing (page 150)

Part 1

Question 1 (essay)
Style: formal
Content: **General:** answer the question about how students can learn something about different types of work, with examples and reasons for all your opinions.
  1 offering to do voluntary work, which is unpaid
  2 watching videos about different jobs online
  3 another point to support your answer (different from 1 and 2)

Part 2

Question 2 (article)
Style: formal
Content: 1 describe some customs or traditions in your country (e.g. festivals, celebrations, dance, food)
  2 say where and when tourists might be able to enjoy them

Question 3 (email)
Style: informal
Content: 1 describe the type of music young people in your country listen to, and say whether you think all young people all over the world listen to the same bands
  2 explain how much of their free time teenagers spend at home, and where they go to have fun

Question 4 (report)
Style: formal
Content: 1 mention the main topics that the sports celebrity talked about
  2 say whether the visit was useful for the students and why
  3 say whether you think other celebrities should be invited and why

Test 8: Listening (page 152)

Part 1

1	A	2	B	3	C	4	B
5	B	6	A	7	C	8	A

Part 2: Competition for young composers

9 personal details
10 workshop
11 instrument(s)
12 professional
13 guitar
14 five/5
15 originality
16 computer screen
17 (the) 22nd (of) June
18 City Hall

Part 3

19	G	20	A	21	F	22	B	23	E

Part 4

24	B	25	C	26	B	27	C
28	A	29	C	30	A		